THIS BOOK BELONGS TO:

_____

Christmas 2013

2013
CHRISTMAS
WITH
Southern Living

2013
CHRISTMAS

WITH

Southern Living

The ultimate guide to holiday cooking & decorating

Oxmoor House

Welcome

It's that joyous time of year again—time to unwrap boxes of sparkling ornaments, prepare delicious goodies from your kitchen for friends and family, plan the holiday feast, and bedeck your home with festive decorations. This year's edition of *Christmas with Southern Living* helps you do all that and much more!

These pages are filled with more than 100 new recipes everyone will love. Whether you're searching for a menu for Christmas morning brunch or one that will bring luck in the New Year, we have you covered. Need a cookie recipe to please Santa? You'll find a jarful for all the days in December leading up to the big day. You'll also find decadent desserts, delicious sides, impressive main dishes, and even bread recipes for every occasion.

We've gathered lots of new ideas for decking the halls. Get inspired by a Christmas carol and add bright copper kettles or warm woolen mittens to spruce up your home. Tuck in some rustic elements on the tree and the holiday table for a home-style feel. You'll love our yuletide decorations that bring a hint of the season to bookcases and shelves.

We hope this book inspires and brings happiness to your holiday. Thanks for allowing us to share the season with you.

Wishing you the merriest of Christmases,

Ashley Strickland Freeman

Ashley Strickland Freeman
EDITOR

CONTENTS

Entertain

WHETHER YOU'RE PLANNING A BIG HOLIDAY
FEAST OR A SMALL FAMILY GATHERING,
YOU'LL FIND THE PERFECT MENU HERE.

Casual Holiday Brunch

Who says that you have to cook fancy feasts during the holidays? Start your holiday off right with these casual brunch ideas. Sleep late and skip the hustle and bustle of preparing three meals…keep it simple with these holiday takes on ordinary brunch menus.

MENU

Winter Citrus Mocktail

Cream Liqueur-Spiked Coffee

Cane Syrup-and-Black Pepper Bacon

Baked Eggs with Tomato-Pesto Sauce

Winter Fruit Salad

Sage Biscuits and Sausage Gravy

serves 6

Winter Citrus Mocktail

Makes: 6 servings
Hands-On Time: 16 min. Total Time: 1 hour, 16 min.

This refreshing mocktail is made with one of winter's prized fruits: the blood orange. The tart-sweet flavor of its scarlet-hued flesh—combined with thyme-infused simple syrup and aromatic bitters, then topped off with sparkling water—makes a delicious and refreshing nonalcoholic beverage with a pleasantly bitter undertone.

- 1 cup sugar
- 6 thyme sprigs
  Ice cubes
- 3 cups fresh or refrigerated blood orange juice
- 1½ tsp. aromatic bitters
- 2 cups lemon-flavored sparkling water
  Garnish: fresh thyme sprigs

1. Bring sugar and 1 cup water to a boil in a medium saucepan over medium-high heat. Boil, stirring often, 1 minute or until sugar is dissolved and mixture is clear. Remove from heat; add thyme sprigs, and cool completely (about 1 hour). Remove and discard thyme.
2. Fill 6 (12-oz.) glasses with ice cubes, filling each three-fourths full. Add 2 Tbsp. thyme simple syrup, ½ cup blood orange juice, ¼ tsp. aromatic bitters, and ⅓ cup sparkling water to each glass; stir.

QUICK & EASY
Cream Liqueur-Spiked Coffee

(pictured on page 17)

Makes: 8 servings
Hands-On Time: 7 min. Total Time: 17 min.

Decadent spiked coffee gets its punch from Amarula, a South African cream liqueur made from oak-aged Marula fruit. This now widely available liqueur has a subtle tropical fruit and caramel flavor.

- 1 cup medium-roast ground coffee
- 1 cup heavy cream
- 2 Tbsp. sugar
- 2 cups Amarula cream liqueur
- 8 tsp. caramel topping

1. Place ground coffee in a coffee filter. Brew coffee in a 12-cup coffeemaker according to manufacturer's instructions using 8 cups water.
2. Beat cream until foamy; gradually add sugar, beating until soft peaks form.
3. Pour coffee into 8 mugs; stir ¼ cup Amarula into each mug. Top each serving with whipped cream, and drizzle with caramel topping.

Cane Syrup-and-Black Pepper Bacon

(pictured on pages 10 and 11)

Makes: 6 servings
Hands-On Time: 9 min. Total Time: 42 min.

This over-the-top bacon is easy to make, and a foil-lined pan makes cleanup a cinch. Tuck bacon strips into a bowl of steaming hot grits for a savory sensation.

- 1 (1-lb.) package thick hickory-smoked bacon slices
- ¼ cup coarsely ground black pepper
- ½ cup cane syrup

1. Preheat oven to 375°. Place bacon in a single layer on a large wire rack in a half-sheet pan lined with heavy-duty aluminum foil. Sprinkle bacon with pepper, pressing gently to adhere.
2. Bake at 375° for 20 minutes. Drizzle bacon with syrup. Bake 13 more minutes or until bacon is crisp.

Oh What Fun! Coffee Bar

Make spirits bright on a cold winter morning with a decked-out coffee bar!

FRESH WHIPPED CREAM

CHOCOLATE SHAVINGS

CINNAMON AND SUGAR

PEPPERMINT STICKS

HAZELNUT, ALMOND, AND COFFEE LIQUEURS

CHOPPED TOFFEE

CRYSTALLIZED GINGER

Baked Eggs with Tomato-Pesto Sauce

Makes: 6 servings
Hands-On Time: 10 min. Total Time: 43 min.

This dish is similar to huevos rancheros, but with an Italian twist.

- 2 garlic cloves, pressed
- 1 Tbsp. olive oil
- 1 (28-oz.) can whole San Marzano tomatoes, chopped
- ³/₄ tsp. table salt, divided
- ³/₄ tsp. freshly ground black pepper, divided
- 12 large eggs
- ¹/₃ cup jarred pesto
- ¹/₃ cup (1¹/₂ oz.) freshly shredded Parmigiano-Reggiano cheese
- 1 Tbsp. chopped fresh basil

1. Preheat oven to 400°. Sauté garlic in hot oil in a medium saucepan over medium heat 1 minute or until golden. Add tomatoes, ¹/₂ tsp. salt, and ¹/₂ tsp. black pepper; bring to a boil over medium-high heat. Reduce heat, and simmer, stirring occasionally, 15 minutes or until sauce slightly thickens.

2. Divide sauce among 6 (6-inch) lightly greased cast-iron skillets or between 2 (8-inch) lightly greased square baking dishes. Break 2 eggs into each skillet or 6 eggs into each baking dish; sprinkle eggs with remaining ¹/₄ tsp. salt and ¹/₄ tsp. black pepper. Dollop pesto around eggs, and sprinkle with cheese.

3. Bake at 400° for 10 minutes or to desired degree of doneness. Sprinkle with basil.

Winter Fruit Salad

Makes: 6 to 8 servings
Hands-On Time: 15 min. Total Time: 15 min.

Vanilla bean paste can be found online or in gourmet food stores. You can also scrape the seeds from half of a vanilla bean, or use 1 tsp. vanilla extract, if desired.

2 navel oranges, peeled and cut crosswise into 1/4-inch slices
2 red grapefruit, peeled and cut crosswise into 1/4-inch slices
1 Fuyu persimmon, peeled and cut crosswise into 1/2-inch slices
1 fresh pineapple, peeled, cored, and cut crosswise into 1/4-inch slices
3 kiwifruit, peeled and sliced
2 clementines, sectioned
1 (4.3-oz.) container pomegranate seeds (3/4 cup)
1 Tbsp. pure maple syrup
4 tsp. fresh lemon juice
1/2 tsp. poppy seeds
1/8 tsp. kosher salt
1/8 tsp. vanilla bean paste
1/4 cup canola oil

1. Arrange orange, grapefruit, persimmon, and pineapple slices on a serving platter, overlapping slightly. Top with kiwifruit slices and clementine sections; sprinkle with pomegranate seeds.
2. Whisk together maple syrup and next 4 ingredients in a medium bowl. Add oil in a slow, steady stream, whisking constantly until smooth. Drizzle vinaigrette over fruit. Serve immediately, or cover and chill until ready to serve.

Sage Biscuits and Sausage Gravy

Makes: 8 servings
Hands-On Time: 22 min. Total Time: 35 min.

Fresh sage added to these classic buttermilk biscuits marries nicely with the pork sausage, which is typically flavored with a bit of the herb.

- 2 cups self-rising flour
- 2 Tbsp. sugar
- 1 Tbsp. finely chopped fresh sage
- 3/4 tsp. table salt, divided
- 1/2 tsp. freshly ground black pepper, divided
- 1/4 cup cold butter, cut up
- 3/4 cup buttermilk
- 3/4 cup whipping cream
- 2 cups milk
- 1 lb. mild ground pork sausage
- 2 Tbsp. all-purpose flour
- 1/4 tsp. ground red pepper (optional)

1. Preheat oven to 475°. Whisk together self-rising flour, sugar, sage, 1/2 tsp. salt, and 1/4 tsp. black pepper in a large bowl. Cut butter into flour mixture with a pastry blender or fork until crumbly. Add buttermilk and cream, stirring just until dry ingredients are moistened.

2. Turn dough out onto a lightly floured surface, and knead lightly 3 or 4 times. Pat or roll dough to 1/2-inch thickness; cut with a 31/2-inch round cutter, and place on a lightly greased baking sheet.

3. Bake at 475° for 13 minutes or until golden brown.

4. Meanwhile, cook milk in a heavy nonaluminum saucepan over medium heat, stirring often, 6 to 8 minutes or just until bubbles appear (do not boil); remove from heat.

5. Brown sausage in a large skillet over medium-high heat, stirring often, 6 minutes or until sausage crumbles and is no longer pink. Sprinkle all-purpose flour over sausage in skillet; cook 1 minute, stirring constantly. Gradually add warm milk, stirring constantly. Stir in remaining 1/4 tsp. salt, remaining 1/4 tsp. black pepper, and, if desired, ground red pepper. Bring mixture to a boil over medium-high heat. Reduce heat, and simmer, stirring constantly, 5 minutes or until thickened. Spoon gravy over split biscuits.

Traditional Holiday Supper

The holidays are filled with traditions centered on family, friends, and food. Spread cheer with time-honored recipes at your next traditional holiday supper. Gather loved ones for a memorable festive feast featuring recipes with a new twist on holiday classics such as fresh-baked ham with cranberries and warm, yeasty rolls with a Southern surprise—sweet potatoes!

MENU

Champagne Cocktail

Mini Brie en Croûte

Spiced Cranberry Ham

Sweet Potato Horseradish Gratin

Southern Green Beans

Sweet Potato Cloverleaf Rolls

Cranberry Congealed Salad

Aunt Irene's Squash Casserole Remix

Stacked Apples

Coconut Cake

serves 10 to 12

Champagne Cocktail

Makes: 10 servings
Hands-On Time: 5 min. Total Time: 5 min.

This simple Champagne cocktail is a perfect aperitif for a holiday meal. The St. Germain liqueur, made from elderflower blossoms, gives this bubbly drink a delicate hint of tropical and citrus fruits. In a pinch, this cocktail also can be made with equal parts Lillet Blanc and Champagne or sparkling wine with a few dashes of aromatic orange bitters.

- 2 cups elderflower liqueur
- 2 cups Lillet Blanc
- 1 (750-milliliter) bottle chilled brut Champagne or sparkling wine
  - Garnish: lemon peel strips

1. Stir together elderflower liqueur and Lillet Blanc in a pitcher. Chill at least 2 hours or until ready to serve.
2. Divide chilled liqueur mixture evenly among 10 (6-oz.) Champagne flutes. Top each with chilled Champagne.

Mini Brie en Croûte

Makes: 18 servings
Hands-On Time: 40 min. Total Time: 1 hour

These appetizers are a miniature version of the traditional wheel of Brie encased in puff pastry.

- 1 (17.3-oz.) package frozen puff pastry sheets, thawed
- 1 (7-oz.) Brie round, cut into 1-inch pieces
- 6 Tbsp. seedless raspberry jam
- 1/2 cup sweetened dried cranberries
- 2/3 cup sliced almonds, toasted and divided
- 1 large egg

1. Preheat oven to 400°. Working with 1 sheet at a time, roll puff pastry into a 12- x 10-inch rectangle. Cut into 9 small rectangles. Place 1 piece of cheese in center of each rectangle; top each with 1 tsp. jam. Sprinkle rectangles evenly with half of cranberries and 2 1/2 Tbsp. almonds. Repeat with remaining puff pastry sheet, cheese, jam, cranberries, and 2 1/2 Tbsp. almonds.
2. Whisk together egg and 1 Tbsp. water. Working with 1 rectangle at a time, brush edges with egg wash. Pull corners of pastry together over filling, pinching edges to seal. Place on ungreased baking sheet. Repeat with remaining pastry rectangles. Brush tops of bundles with remaining egg wash, and sprinkle with remaining almonds.
3. Bake at 400° for 17 to 18 minutes or until puffed and golden. Serve warm.

NOTE: If pastries open slightly during baking, gently pinch edges back together immediately after removing from oven.

Sweet Potato Horseradish Gratin

Makes: 12 servings
Hands-On Time: 35 min. Total Time: 1 hour, 40 min.

Sweet and savory all at the same time, this dish is sure to become a family favorite!

- 8 cups (1/8-inch-thick) sliced sweet potatoes
- 3 Tbsp. fresh thyme leaves
- 1 (5-oz.) package shredded Parmesan cheese
- 2 cups heavy cream
- 3 Tbsp. prepared horseradish
- 1 tsp. table salt
- 1 tsp. freshly ground black pepper
- 1 large egg yolk

1. Preheat oven to 375°. Cook sweet potatoes in boiling salted water to cover 3 minutes or until crisp-tender; drain. Place sweet potato slices in a single layer on paper towels; let cool 10 minutes.
2. Arrange one-fourth of sweet potatoes in a lightly greased 13- x 9-inch baking dish. Sprinkle with half of thyme. Top with another one-fourth of sweet potatoes and half of Parmesan cheese. Arrange another one-fourth of sweet potatoes over Parmesan cheese. Spinkle with remaining thyme. Top with remaining sweet potatoes and remaining Parmesan cheese. Whisk together heavy cream and next 4 ingredients; pour over sweet potato mixture.
3. Cover loosely with aluminum foil, and bake at 375° for 35 minutes. Uncover and bake 30 more minutes or until top is lightly browned.

Set a Merry Table

CALL THEM BY NAME
Make family members feel like honored guests with handwritten place cards nestled in a mini vase of flowers at each setting.

SILVER TIDINGS
Add some sparkle to your tablescape by bringing out vintage silver candlesticks, mix-and-match glittery-grey linens, and silver-rimmed glasses for toasting.

OH, CHRISTMAS TREE
Tuck in small branches of evergreen here and there to bring the wintry-woodland feeling indoors.

Spiced Cranberry Ham

Makes: 10 to 12 servings
Hands-On Time: 8 min. Total Time: 3 hours, 18 min.

The spiced-sugar coating and cranberry-honey mixture help keep the ham moist while adding lots of flavor.

- 1 (10- to 12-lb.) fully cooked, bone-in whole ham
- 2/3 cup jellied cranberry sauce
- 3 Tbsp. honey
- 1 cup firmly packed dark brown sugar
- 1 tsp. ground cinnamon
- 3/4 tsp. ground ginger
- 3/4 tsp. ground cloves
- 1/2 tsp. ground nutmeg

1. Preheat oven to 325°. Remove skin from ham, and trim fat to 1/4-inch thickness. Make shallow cuts in fat 1 inch apart in a diamond pattern. Place ham, fat side up, on a rack in an aluminum foil-lined shallow roasting pan.

2. Bake at 325° on lowest oven rack for 1 1/2 hours. Remove ham from oven; leave oven on.

3. Whisk together cranberry sauce and honey; brush ham with glaze. Stir together brown sugar and next 4 ingredients; press into glaze, coating ham.

4. Return ham to oven; bake at 325° for 1 hour and 20 minutes or until a meat thermometer registers 140°. (Cover ham with foil during the last 30 minutes, if necessary, to prevent excessive browning.) Let stand 15 minutes before carving.

Southern Green Beans

Makes: 16 servings
Hands-On Time: 30 min. Total Time: 1 hour, 20 min.

For a pretty presentation, trim just the stem ends of the green beans.

- 6 bacon slices, chopped
- 1 large onion, chopped
- 1/8 tsp. dried crushed red pepper
- 6 cups low-sodium fat-free chicken broth
- 3 lb. fresh green beans, trimmed and halved
- 1 tsp. table salt

Cook bacon, stirring often, in a large Dutch oven over medium heat 6 minutes or until crisp. Add onion and red pepper, and cook, stirring occasionally, 5 minutes. Add chicken broth, stirring to loosen particles from bottom of pan. Add green beans and salt; bring to a boil. Cover, reduce heat, and simmer 50 minutes or until green beans are very tender, stirring occasionally.

Sweet Potato Cloverleaf Rolls

Makes: 2¹/₂ dozen
Hands-On Time: 47 min. Total Time: 3 hours, 47 min.

A favorite for traditional holiday suppers, these tender cloverleaf rolls slathered with Orange-Honey Butter don't last long.

- 2 (¹/₄-oz.) envelopes active dry yeast
- 1 cup warm milk (100° to 110°)
- 1 Tbsp. granulated sugar
- 4 to 4¹/₂ cups all-purpose flour, divided
- ³/₄ cup mashed cooked sweet potato (1 medium)
- ¹/₃ cup firmly packed brown sugar
- ¹/₃ cup unsalted butter, softened
- 1 Tbsp. orange zest
- 1¹/₄ tsp. table salt
- 1 large egg, lightly beaten
- ¹/₄ cup unsalted butter, melted
- Orange-Honey Butter

1. Stir together yeast, warm milk, and granulated sugar in the bowl of a heavy-duty electric stand mixer; let stand 5 minutes.
2. Add 2 cups flour to bowl, and beat at low speed, using dough hook attachment, until combined. Add sweet potato and next 5 ingredients; beat at medium-low speed until well blended, stopping to scrape down sides as needed. Gradually add 2 cups flour, beating until dough begins to leave the sides of bowl and pulls together and becomes soft and smooth.
3. Place dough in a well-greased bowl, turning to grease top. Cover with plastic wrap, and let rise in a warm place (85°), free from drafts, 1¹/₂ to 2 hours or until doubled in bulk.
4. Punch dough down; turn out onto a lightly floured surface, and knead 8 to 10 times.
5. Lightly grease muffin pans. Shape dough into 90 (1-inch) balls; place 3 balls in each cup of muffin pans. Cover and let rise in a warm place (85°), free from drafts, 1 hour or until doubled in bulk.
6. Preheat oven to 375°. Bake at 375° for 10 to 12 minutes or until golden brown. Brush with melted butter. Serve with Orange-Honey Butter.

Orange-Honey Butter

Makes: 1¹/₃ cups
Hands-On Time: 3 min. Total Time: 3 min.

- 1 cup butter, softened
- ¹/₂ cup honey
- 1 Tbsp. orange zest
- ¹/₄ tsp. orange extract

Stir together all ingredients in a small bowl. Serve at room temperature.

Cranberry Congealed Salad

Makes: 12 servings
Hands-On Time: 13 min. Total Time: 5 hours, 13 min.

The crunch of celery, apple, and pecans in this salad is a nice contrast to the sweet-tart cranberry mixture.

- 4 **cups fresh cranberries**
- 2 **cups sugar**
- 1/4 **tsp. table salt**
- 2 **(3-oz.) packages strawberry-flavored gelatin**
- 1 1/2 **cups finely chopped celery**
- 1 1/2 **cups peeled chopped Fuji apple (1 large)**
- 1 **cup chopped pecans**
- 1 **Tbsp. orange zest**
- **Garnish: celery leaves**

1. Combine cranberries and 2 1/2 cups water in a large saucepan; bring to a boil. Reduce heat, and simmer 3 minutes, stirring often, until cranberry skins begin to split. Stir in sugar and salt; cook 1 minute, stirring until sugar dissolves.

2. Remove pan from heat; add gelatin, stirring 1 minute or until gelatin dissolves. Chill mixture 1 hour or until consistency of unbeaten egg whites. Stir in celery and next 3 ingredients.

3. Spoon mixture into 12 (6-oz.) lightly greased individual molds or a 9-cup ring mold. Cover and chill 4 to 6 hours or until firm. Unmold salad onto platter.

Aunt Irene's Squash Casserole Remix

(pictured on page 23)

Makes: 12 servings
Hands-On Time: 56 min. Total Time: 1 hour, 36 min.

This family-favorite casserole was passed from our Assistant Test Kitchen Director Julie Christopher's Aunt Irene to Julie's mom, then to Julie, who now prepares the dish for the family's big holiday meal. Julie increased the original recipe and replaced frozen squash with fresh, since it's now readily available in December.

- $3^3/_4$ lb. yellow squash, sliced (12 cups)
- 12 oz. processed cheese (such as Velveeta), cut into $1/_2$-inch cubes
- $1^1/_2$ cups butter
- 3 large onions, chopped ($7^1/_4$ cups)
- 3 sleeves saltine crackers, coarsely crushed

1. Preheat oven to 350°. Combine squash and $1/_2$ cup water in a 6-qt. Dutch oven. Cover and bring to a boil over medium heat, stirring often. Reduce heat, and simmer, covered, 15 to 20 minutes or until tender, stirring occasionally. Add cheese, pressing with a potato masher until cheese melts.

2. Meanwhile, melt butter in a large skillet over medium heat; add onion, and sauté 15 minutes or until tender. Remove from heat; stir in crackers.

3. Stir half of onion mixture into squash mixture. Spoon squash mixture into a lightly greased 13- x 9-inch baking dish. Spread remaining onion mixture over squash mixture in dish.

4. Bake at 350° for 35 minutes or until bubbly and topping is golden brown. Let stand 10 minutes before serving.

MAKE AHEAD: Cook squash and onion mixtures through Step 2, but do not stir in crackers. Place squash mixture and onion mixture in separate bowls; cover and chill. When ready to bake, preheat oven to 350°, and reheat squash and onion mixtures in microwave. Stir crackers into onion mixture, and proceed as directed in recipe.

Stacked Apples

Makes: 12 servings
Hands-On Time: 1 hour, 12 min. Total Time: 1 hour, 12 min.

This versatile dish can be served warm or chilled, as a side or a dessert. We recommend making it the day before and chilling overnight. The apples are delicious the next day, whether you warm them or eat them cold.

- 3 cups sugar
- 1 cup fresh lemon juice
- 2 Tbsp. butter, melted
- 3 large eggs, lightly beaten
- 5 Fuji apples, peeled and cored
- 1 cup all-purpose flour
- $3/_4$ tsp. baking soda
- $3/_4$ tsp. table salt
- 1 cup buttermilk
- 1 large egg, lightly beaten
- 3 Tbsp. canola oil
  Additional canola oil

1. Combine sugar, lemon juice, butter, and 3 eggs in a large saucepan; bring to a boil over medium heat, stirring constantly. Cook, stirring constantly, 10 minutes or until thickened. Remove from heat; set aside.

2. Cut apples into $1/_2$-inch-thick slices. Combine flour, baking soda, and salt in a large bowl. Whisk together buttermilk, 1 egg, and 3 Tbsp. canola oil; add to flour mixture, whisking just until blended.

3. Pour canola oil to depth of $1/_2$ inch in a large cast-iron skillet. Heat over medium heat to 350°. Dip apples in batter, shaking off excess. Fry apples, in 4 batches, in hot oil 1 to 2 minutes on each side or until golden brown. Drain on a wire rack over paper towels.

4. Layer one-third apples in an ungreased 11- x 7-inch baking dish; spoon one-third reserved lemon juice mixture evenly over apples. Repeat layers twice. Serve warm or chilled.

Coconut Cake

Makes: 14 to 16 servings
Hands-On Time: 26 min. Total Time: 7 hours, 16 min.

*This cake is tall and grand, so you'll need your largest
mixing bowl for folding the egg whites into the batter.*

1½	cups unsalted butter, softened
2²/₃	cups sugar
6	large eggs, separated
1	(21-oz.) bottle cream of coconut, divided
2	tsp. vanilla extract, divided
4	cups all-purpose flour
1½	tsp. baking powder
³/₄	tsp. baking soda
³/₄	tsp. table salt
1½	cups buttermilk
2½	cups heavy cream
	Dash of table salt
4	cups sweetened flaked coconut

1. Preheat oven to 350°. Beat butter and sugar at medium speed with a
heavy-duty electric stand mixer, using paddle attachment, until fluffy. Add
egg yolks, 1½ cups cream of coconut, and 1½ tsp. vanilla, beating until
blended.

2. Whisk together flour and next 3 ingredients; add to butter mixture
alternately with buttermilk, beginning and ending with flour mixture. Beat
at low speed until blended after each addition, stopping to scrape down
bowl as needed. Transfer to a very large bowl.

3. Beat egg whites, using whisk attachment, at high speed until stiff peaks
form (about 2 minutes). Stir one-fourth beaten egg whites into batter; fold
in remaining egg whites.

4. Divide cake batter among 3 greased and floured 9-inch round cake pans
with 2-inch sides. Bake at 350° for 35 to 40 minutes or until a wooden pick
inserted in centers comes out clean. Cool in pans on wire racks 10 minutes;
remove from pans to wire racks, and cool completely (about 1 hour).

5. Beat heavy cream, dash of salt, remaining ½ cup cream of coconut, and
remaining ½ tsp. vanilla at medium speed with an electric mixer until stiff
peaks form (about 3 minutes).

6. Place 1 cake layer on a serving plate or cake stand; spread with 1¼ cups
whipped cream mixture, and sprinkle with ³/₄ cup coconut. Top with
second cake layer; spread with 1¼ cups whipped cream mixture, and
sprinkle with ³/₄ cup coconut. Top with remaining cake layer. Spread
remaining whipped cream mixture over top and sides of cake. Gently
press remaining coconut into whipped cream mixture on top and sides of
cake. Cover and chill 4 to 24 hours. Store cake in refrigerator. Let stand at
room temperature 1 hour before serving.

Feast of 7 Fishes

The Feast of 7 Fishes is an Italian Christmas tradition, originally meaning seven different kinds of seafood, cooked seven different ways. Whether it's boiled, baked, or sautéed; shrimp, clams, or crab; you'll find a cooking style and a type of seafood for everyone!

MENU

Boiled Shrimp with Romesco Sauce

Calamari Salad

*Pan-Seared Swordfish
with Fennel-Caper Sauce*

Baked Clams

*Sautéed Broccoli Rabe
with Bacon and Pine Nuts*

Mixed Shellfish Pasta

Crab Arancini

*Gingered Bread Pudding with
Limoncello Cream Sauce*

serves 6 to 8

Boiled Shrimp with Romesco Sauce

Makes: 8 servings
Hands-On Time: 20 min.
Total Time: 1 hour, 18 min.

Free up kitchen space for the remainder of the menu by prepping this appetizer up to 1 day ahead.

- 2 lemons, halved
- 1 medium onion, quartered
- 1/4 cup dried crushed red pepper
- 1 1/2 tsp. table salt, divided
- 2 lb. unpeeled, large raw shrimp
- 2 medium-size red bell peppers
- 2 cups grape tomatoes
- 3 garlic cloves
- 1/4 cup toasted slivered almonds
- 1/2 cup freshly grated Parmigiano-Reggiano cheese
- 2 Tbsp. olive oil
- 2 Tbsp. sherry vinegar
- 1/2 tsp. smoked paprika
- 2 Tbsp. chopped fresh parsley

1. Preheat oven to 350°. Bring lemons, onion, red pepper, 1 tsp. table salt, and 6 cups water to a boil in a Dutch oven. Add shrimp, and cook 2 minutes. Remove from heat, and let stand 10 minutes. Drain and cool slightly (about 30 minutes). Cover and chill until ready to serve.
2. Meanwhile, preheat broiler with oven rack 5 inches from heat. Broil peppers and tomatoes on an aluminum foil-lined baking sheet 10 minutes or until peppers and tomatoes look blistered, turning peppers every 2 to 3 minutes. Place peppers in a large zip-top plastic freezer bag, reserving pan juices; seal and let stand 10 minutes to loosen skins. Peel peppers; remove and discard seeds.
3. With processor running, drop garlic cloves through food chute, and process until minced. Add toasted almonds, peeled peppers, tomatoes, pan juices, cheese, oil, vinegar, paprika, and remaining 1/2 tsp. salt; process until smooth.
4. Spoon sauce into a bowl; stir in parsley. Cover and chill until ready to serve. Arrange chilled shrimp on a serving platter. Serve with Romesco Sauce.

Calamari Salad

Makes: 12 servings
Hands-On Time: 15 min. Total Time: 2 hours, 15 min.

This salad will be a perfect starter to your feast—fresh, light, and lemony.

- 1 (2.5-lb.) package cleaned calamari (tubes and tentacles), rinsed
- ½ cup fresh lemon juice
- ⅓ cup extra virgin olive oil
- ½ tsp. coarse sea salt
- ½ tsp. freshly ground black pepper
- 2 small garlic cloves, pressed
- ½ cup thinly sliced red onion
- ¾ cup coarsely chopped pitted Sicilian olives or other green olives
- 4 celery ribs with leaves, sliced (2 cups)
- 2 navel oranges, sectioned

1. Cut calamari tubes crosswise into ½-inch rings; leave tentacles intact. Cook calamari in lightly salted boiling water 35 to 40 seconds or just until rings are opaque. Plunge calamari into ice water to stop the cooking process; drain.

2. Whisk together lemon juice and next 4 ingredients in a large bowl; add onion and next 3 ingredients, and toss gently. Add calamari; toss gently to coat. Cover and chill 2 hours.

Pan-Seared Swordfish with Fennel-Caper Sauce

Makes: 8 servings
Hands-On Time: 25 min. Total Time: 25 min.

Halibut, mahi-mahi, or any other firm, white fish can be substituted if you cannot find swordfish.

- 1 small fennel bulb
- 2 Tbsp. olive oil, divided
- 2 garlic cloves, minced
- 1/2 cup dry white wine
- 2 Tbsp. capers
- 1 tsp. lemon zest
- 1 tsp. table salt, divided
- 3/4 tsp. freshly ground black pepper, divided
- 2 Tbsp. butter
- 8 (6-oz.) swordfish steaks

1. Rinse fennel thoroughly. Trim and discard root end of fennel bulb. Trim stalks from bulb, reserving fronds. Slice bulb.

2. Sauté sliced fennel bulb in 2 tsp. hot oil in a medium saucepan over medium-high heat 5 minutes or until lightly browned. Add garlic; sauté 30 seconds. Add wine, capers, lemon zest, 1/2 tsp. salt, and 1/4 tsp. black pepper; bring to simmer, and cook, stirring occasionally, 2 minutes. Remove from heat; stir in butter. Keep warm.

3. Sprinkle both sides of swordfish steaks with remaining 1/2 tsp. salt and 1/2 tsp. black pepper. Heat 2 tsp. oil in a large skillet over medium-high heat; add 4 swordfish steaks to pan, and cook 5 minutes on each side or until fish flakes with a fork. Remove from skillet; keep warm. Repeat procedure with remaining 2 tsp. oil and swordfish steaks. Serve fennel-caper sauce over fish; sprinkle with reserved fennel fronds.

Baked Clams

Makes: 8 servings
Hands-On Time: 30 min. Total Time: 30 min.

For easier shucking, steam clams over simmering water for 1 to 2 minutes or just until their shells barely open. Run a knife or small screwdriver around each shell's edge, and pop it open.

24	small clams in shells, scrubbed
2	large shallots, finely chopped (1/2 cup)
1	small red bell pepper, finely chopped (1 1/4 cups)
4	Tbsp. olive oil, divided
2	garlic cloves, minced
1	cup soft, fresh breadcrumbs
2	Tbsp. chopped fresh oregano
2	Tbsp. chopped fresh parsley
1/4	tsp. table salt
1/8	tsp. dried crushed red pepper

1. Preheat broiler with oven rack 5 1/2 inches from heat. Discard any clams with broken or open shells. Shuck clams, reserving any clam liquid in a small bowl; discard top halves of shells. Loosen clams from bottom shells, leaving shells intact.

2. Sauté shallots and red bell pepper in 3 Tbsp. hot oil in a medium-size nonstick skillet over medium-high heat 6 minutes or until tender. Add garlic; sauté 1 minute. Add breadcrumbs; cook 3 minutes or until lightly browned. Remove from heat; stir in oregano, parsley, salt, crushed red pepper, and reserved clam juice.

3. Arrange clams in a single layer on an aluminum foil-lined baking sheet. Spoon about 2 tsp. breadcrumb mixture onto each clam. Broil clams 2 to 3 minutes or until breadcrumbs are golden brown. Drizzle clams evenly with remaining 1 Tbsp. oil.

Sautéed Broccoli Rabe with Bacon and Pine Nuts
(pictured on page 32)

Makes: 8 servings
Hands-On Time: 17 min. Total Time: 17 min.

Traditionally when the Feast of Seven Fishes is served, a vegetable such as broccoli rabe, Broccolini, or kale is sautéed in oil and served alongside the main dishes.

- ¼ cup balsamic vinegar
- 2 Tbsp. brown sugar
- ½ tsp. table salt
- ½ tsp. freshly ground black pepper
- 3 bunches fresh broccoli rabe (2¼ lb.), chopped (15 cups)
- 4 bacon slices
- ¾ cup vertically sliced onion
- ¼ cup toasted pine nuts

1. Whisk together first 4 ingredients in a small bowl.
2. Cook broccoli rabe in boiling water to cover 2 minutes or until crisp-tender; drain and pat dry with paper towels.
3. Cook bacon in a large skillet over medium-high heat 6 to 8 minutes or until crisp; remove bacon, and drain on paper towels, reserving drippings in skillet. Crumble bacon.
4. Sauté onion in hot drippings 4 minutes. Add broccoli rabe; sauté 2 minutes. Pour vinegar mixture over broccoli rabe; toss well. Remove from heat; sprinkle with toasted pine nuts.

Mixed Shellfish Pasta
(pictured on page 28)

Makes: 8 servings
Hands-On Time: 45 min. Total Time: 45 min.

Clams or lobster would also work in place of any of the shellfish listed here. Preserved lemons add both a briny and tart flavor to this full-bodied sauce. If you're serving this dish as a single entrée rather than part of a full menu, then double the pasta.

- 4 garlic cloves, minced
- 2 large shallots, chopped (½ cup)
- 2 Tbsp. olive oil
- ½ cup pitted niçoise olives, halved
- 1 Tbsp. chopped preserved lemon
- 1 (28-oz.) can San Marzano tomatoes, undrained and chopped
- 1 cup seafood or fish stock
- ½ cup dry vermouth
- ⅓ cup chopped fresh flat-leaf parsley
- ½ tsp. dried crushed red pepper
- 2 bay leaves
- 2 lb. fresh mussels, scrubbed and debearded
- ¾ lb. peeled, large raw shrimp
- 8 large sea scallops
- 1 (9-oz.) package refrigerated linguine
  Freshly grated Parmigiano-Reggiano cheese

1. Sauté garlic and shallots in hot oil in a large Dutch oven over medium heat 2 minutes. Add olives and preserved lemon; sauté 1 minute. Add tomatoes, seafood stock, and next 4 ingredients; bring to a boil. Reduce heat, and simmer 10 minutes.
2. Add mussels, shrimp, and scallops; cover and cook 4 minutes or until shrimp turn pink and mussel shells open. Discard any unopened shells. Remove and discard bay leaves.
3. Cook linguine according to package directions; drain. Serve seafood mixture over pasta with freshly grated Parmigiano-Reggiano cheese.

Crab Arancini
(pictured on page 28)

Makes: 2 dozen
Hands-On Time: 1 hour, 6 min. Total Time: 3 hours, 6 min.

Arancini are fried rice balls coated in breadcrumbs that are often filled with meats, mozzarella cheese, or peas. Their name derives from the Italian word for "little orange," referring to their shape and color.

- 3¾ cups chicken broth
- 1 cup finely chopped onion
- 2 garlic cloves, minced
- ¼ cup olive oil
- 1 cup Arborio rice (short grain)
- ½ cup dry white wine
- ½ tsp. table salt
- ½ tsp. freshly ground black pepper
- 1 lb. fresh lump crabmeat, drained
- ¼ cup freshly grated Romano cheese
- 1 Tbsp. chopped fresh basil
- 1 Tbsp. lemon zest
  Canola oil
- 2 large eggs, lightly beaten
- 2 cups Italian-seasoned breadcrumbs
- 1 (4-oz.) block mozzarella cheese, cut into ½-inch cubes

1. Bring chicken broth to a simmer in a medium saucepan; keep warm over low heat.
2. Sauté onion and garlic in hot oil in a large deep skillet over medium heat 3 minutes or until tender. Add rice; sauté 2 minutes or until toasted. Add wine; cook 1 to 2 minutes or until wine is absorbed. Stir in salt and pepper. Reduce heat to medium-low; add ½ cup hot broth, and cook, stirring constantly, until liquid is absorbed. Repeat procedure with remaining broth, ½ cup at a time, making sure the liquid has been absorbed each time before adding more. (Total cooking time is 25 to 30 minutes.) Remove from heat; stir in crabmeat, Romano cheese, basil, and lemon zest. Transfer to a large bowl; cover and chill 2 hours or overnight.
3. Pour oil to a depth of 3 inches in a 6-qt. Dutch oven or large deep skillet; heat to 350°.
4. Stir eggs and ½ cup breadcrumbs into risotto in bowl. Shape mixture into 24 (2-inch) balls. Press 1 mozzarella cube into center of each ball, making sure it's covered by risotto mixture. Place remaining 1½ cups breadcrumbs in a shallow bowl; roll balls in breadcrumbs.
5. Fry risotto balls, in batches, 2 to 3 minutes or until golden brown. Drain on a wire rack over paper towels. Serve warm.

Gingered Bread Pudding with Limoncello Cream Sauce

Makes: 12 servings
Hands-On Time: 18 min. Total Time: 1 hour, 33 min.

Traditional bread puddings are served with a whiskey sauce, but limoncello, a lemon-flavored Italian liqueur, pairs perfectly.

- 4 large eggs
- 3 cups milk
- 1 cup half-and-half
- 1 cup firmly packed light brown sugar
- 3 Tbsp. butter, melted
- 2 tsp. lemon zest
- 1/4 tsp. table salt
- 1/4 cup chopped crystallized ginger
- 1 (12-oz.) French bread loaf, cut into 1-inch cubes (12 cups)
- 1 cup golden raisins
  Limoncello Cream Sauce

1. Preheat oven to 325°. Whisk together first 7 ingredients in a large bowl; stir in crystallized ginger. Add bread cubes, stirring to coat. Let stand 10 minutes. Stir in raisins. Spoon mixture into a lightly greased 13- x 9-inch baking dish.

2. Bake at 325° for 1 hour or until set. Let cool 15 minutes before cutting into squares. Serve with Limoncello Cream Sauce.

Limoncello Cream Sauce

Makes: 1³/₄ cups
Hands-On Time: 9 min. Total Time: 9 min.

- 1/2 cup butter
- 1 cup sugar
- 1/2 cup half-and-half
- 1/4 cup limoncello

Cook butter and sugar in a medium saucepan over medium-low heat, stirring constantly, 3 minutes or until smooth. Stir in half-and-half. Cook, stirring constantly, 5 minutes or until thickened. Remove from heat; stir in limoncello.

MENU

Easy Hoppin' John

*Pork Chops with Bourbon-
Rosemary-Mustard Sauce*

*Kale Salad with
Hot Bacon Dressing*

Pecan Cornbread

Fig Upside-Down Cake

serves 4 to 6

Good Luck New Year

Legend says what you do on New Year's Day determines what you do for the rest of the year, so spend time with friends and family by enjoying a hearty feast. These foods are said to bring good luck in the New Year, so eat up and enjoy!

Easy Hoppin' John

Makes: 4 to 6 servings
Hands-On Time: 14 min. Total Time: 14 min.

Boil-in-bag rice, canned peas, and fully cooked bacon keep your kitchen work to a minimum in this classic dish that's good for lunch or dinner.

    1 (3.5-oz.) package boil-in-bag whole grain brown
      or white rice
  1/2 tsp. table salt
    4 fully cooked bacon slices
    3 Tbsp. butter
  3/4 cup chopped celery
  3/4 cup finely chopped red bell pepper
  1/2 cup chopped onion
    4 garlic cloves, minced
    1 (15-oz.) can black-eyed peas, drained and rinsed
    1 tsp. Asian Sriracha hot chili sauce
  1/4 tsp. freshly ground black pepper
      Garnish: celery leaves

1. Cook rice according to package directions, adding 1/2 tsp. salt to water; drain well. Heat bacon according to package directions; crumble.
2. Melt butter in a large skillet over medium heat; add celery and next 3 ingredients, and sauté 5 to 7 minutes or until vegetables are tender. Stir in rice, peas, hot chili sauce, and black pepper; sauté 1 to 2 minutes or until thoroughly heated. Sprinkle with crumbled bacon.

Pork Chops with Bourbon-Rosemary-Mustard Sauce

Makes: 6 servings
Hands-On Time: 24 min. Total Time: 34 min.

Finishing the pork chops in the oven ensures juicy chops that aren't overbrowned on the outside.

- 6 (1-inch-thick) bone-in center-cut pork chops
- 1/2 tsp. table salt
- 1 tsp. freshly ground black pepper, divided
- 2 Tbsp. butter
- 1 Tbsp. olive oil
- 2 garlic cloves, minced
- 1/2 cup chicken broth
- 1/4 cup bourbon or whiskey
- 1/4 cup country-style Dijon mustard
- 1/4 cup heavy cream
- 1 Tbsp. chopped fresh rosemary

1. Preheat oven to 400°. Sprinkle pork chops with salt and 1/2 tsp. black pepper.
2. Melt 1 Tbsp. butter with 1 1/2 tsp. oil in a large ovenproof skillet. Brown half of pork chops 2 to 3 minutes on each side. Remove from skillet to a plate. Repeat procedure with remaining butter, oil, and pork chops. Arrange all pork chops in skillet, overlapping slightly; bake at 400° for 10 minutes or until meat thermometer inserted in thickest portion of chops registers 155°. Remove pork chops from skillet to a platter, reserving drippings in skillet. Cover chops, and let stand 10 minutes or until meat thermometer inserted in thickest portion of chops registers 160°.
3. Add garlic to drippings in skillet; sauté over medium heat 1 minute. Add broth, bourbon, mustard, cream, and remaining 1/2 tsp. black pepper. Cook, stirring occasionally, 4 minutes or until sauce is reduced to 2/3 cup. Stir in rosemary; cook 1 minute. Serve sauce over pork chops.

Kale Salad with Hot Bacon Dressing

(pictured on page 39)

Makes: 6 to 8 servings
Hands-On Time: 20 min. Total Time: 20 min.

Popular in Italian cuisine, lacinato kale has long, slightly bumpy dark blue-green leaves and a milder flavor than the curly variety.

- 2 bunches lacinato kale (about 1 lb.)
- 6 bacon slices
- 1 shallot, minced
- 1 garlic clove, minced
- 1/3 cup apple cider vinegar
- 1 Tbsp. honey
- 1/2 tsp. table salt
- 1/4 tsp. freshly ground black pepper
- 1/4 cup freshly grated Romano cheese
- 2 hard-cooked eggs, peeled and finely shredded

1. Trim and discard thick stems from kale; thinly slice leaves, and place in a large bowl.
2. Cook bacon in a large skillet over medium-high heat 8 minutes or until crisp; remove bacon, and drain on paper towels, reserving 3 Tbsp. drippings in skillet. Crumble bacon.
3. Sauté shallot and garlic in hot drippings 2 minutes or until just tender. Stir in vinegar, honey, salt, black pepper, and 1/4 cup water; bring to a boil. Remove from heat; stir in bacon.
4. Drizzle vinegar mixture over kale, and sprinkle with cheese; toss to coat. Top with shredded eggs.

Pecan Cornbread

(pictured on page 36)

Makes: 6 to 8 servings
Hands-On Time: 5 min. Total Time: 35 min.

Serve this cornbread with pepper jelly and butter.

- 1 cup finely chopped pecans
- 1/3 cup shortening
- 2 cups yellow self-rising cornmeal mix
- 1 Tbsp. sugar
- 1/2 tsp. ground red pepper
- 2 cups buttermilk
- 1 large egg

1. Preheat oven to 350°. Bake pecans in a single layer in a shallow pan 5 to 8 minutes or until toasted and fragrant, stirring halfway through. Remove pecans from oven, and increase temperature to 425°.
2. Melt shortening in a 10-inch cast-iron skillet in oven 5 minutes. Stir together cornmeal mix, sugar, and ground red pepper in a medium bowl. Whisk together buttermilk and egg; add to cornmeal mixture, stirring just until moistened. Stir in pecans.

3. Remove skillet from oven; tilt skillet to coat, and pour shortening into batter, stirring until blended. Immediately pour batter into hot skillet.
4. Bake at 425° for 25 minutes or until edges are golden brown.

NOTE: If you have any cornbread left over and about 1 1/2 cups of Easy Hoppin' John (page 38) remaining, you can make a quick-and-easy cornbread salad. Crumble cornbread to measure 3 cups, and stir into leftover Easy Hoppin' John. Add 1/3 cup mayonnaise and 1/3 cup Ranch dressing, stirring until just moistened. Serve immediately, or cover and chill salad until ready to serve.

Fig Upside-Down Cake

Makes: 6 to 8 servings
Hands-On Time: 28 min. Total Time: 1 hour, 8 min.

Port is a blend of a still wine, typically red, and brandy. Ruby port gets its name from the distinct ruby color created from the mix of grapes used to make this variety. Although the port is an exceptional addition to the whipped cream, and pairs beautifully with the cake, it can be omitted.

- 1/2 cup butter
- 1 cup firmly packed brown sugar
- 12 fresh Brown Turkey or Mission figs, halved
- 1/2 cup chopped walnuts
- 2 large eggs, separated
- 1 large egg yolk
- 1 cup granulated sugar
- 1 cup all-purpose flour
- 1 tsp. baking powder
- 1 tsp. chopped fresh rosemary
- 1 tsp. lemon zest
- 1/4 tsp. table salt
- 1/4 cup milk
- 1/2 tsp. vanilla extract
- 3/4 cup whipping cream
- 2 Tbsp. ruby port (optional)

1. Preheat oven to 350°. Melt butter in a 10-inch cast-iron skillet over medium-low heat; sprinkle brown sugar over butter. Remove from heat. Arrange figs, cut sides down, over sugar mixture; sprinkle with walnuts.
2. Beat 3 egg yolks at high speed with an electric mixer until thick and pale; gradually add 1 cup granulated sugar, beating well. Stir together flour and next 4 ingredients; add to egg mixture alternately with milk, beginning and ending with flour mixture. Stir in vanilla.
3. Beat egg whites at high speed with an electric mixer until stiff peaks form; fold egg whites into batter. Pour batter over figs in skillet.
4. Bake at 350° for 38 to 40 minutes or until a wooden pick inserted in center comes out clean. Cool in skillet on a wire rack 10 minutes; invert cake onto a serving platter, scraping any syrup from bottom of skillet onto cake.
5. Beat whipping cream and port until soft peaks form. Serve cake warm or at room temperature with whipped cream.

Decorate

EASY AND BEAUTIFUL, THESE FESTIVE DECORATIONS
WILL ADD CHEER ALL THROUGH THE HOUSE.

brown paper packages

Favorite Things

Who says holiday decor has to be all red and green or tinsel and holly? Incorporate everyday items and beloved collections into your decorating this year for looks that are fresh and festive.

raindrops and roses

bright copper

warm woolen mittens

{1}

Raindrops and Roses

1 DINING TABLE DRAMA
Handblown glass "raindrops" drip from arching, winged elm branches, which add height and interest to a mass of roses in a sterling vessel. Flocked crystal sprays lend an ethereal quality to this sophisticated holiday table.

2 PRETTY POSIES
More roses tucked into gleaming julep cups with greenery brighten a windowsill. Get frosted panes and mirrors even in the warmest climates with ice crystal spray, available at crafts stores.

3 GLISTENING GLASS
Hollow glass drops are suspended from lengths of pearly organza ribbon that add to the shimmer. Use clear fishing line for drops that appear in free fall.

4 BOUNTIFUL BLOOMS
Roses in sorbet and sherbet hues provide a wave of lovely contrasts, but a mass of blooms in a single hue—scarlet or white—would be equally stunning. A footed container with graceful curves is an elegant anchor.

{4}

Bright Copper

A less common holiday hue, copper seems lit from within. Its shimmering warmth works beautifully with deep greens and rich woods. Kitchen items in copper, such as miniature pots, tumblers, ladles, and pitchers, take center stage with ornaments, candles, berries, and greenery in this glowing sideboard display.

{1}

{2}

{3}

1 SIMPLE THINGS

Stack metallic ornaments in a copper bowl for an easy yet elegant arrangement. Wind shiny ribbon around the baubles and fill in gaps with feathery evergreen sprigs for an all-season-long decoration.

2 BRIGHT SPOTS

Use vivid red holly berries to bring a spark of color to a bronze-hued display. Tuck a few berry branches into small pots to add bright pops. For a bold statement, gather several stems into a bouquet for a large vase.

3 FESTIVE FLICKER

Amp up the holiday sparkle with candlelight. Shaped candles, like the Christmas trees shown here, provide twinkle and festivity. Petite votive candles give the entire sideboard a warm glow.

Warm Woolen Mittens

Shop the attic, closet, or cedar chest for old blankets, threadbare mittens, knitted hats, and scarves, and then weave them into your holiday decor. Artfully arranged with other passed-down heirlooms, they create a focal point that is both a walk down memory lane and a conversation piece for visiting family and friends.

1 **STOCKING STAND-INS**
Handmade mittens hang from antique milk pails, which act as stand-ins for traditional stockings.

2 **FELT FLYER**
Overstuffed felt bird ornaments are tailor-made for bare-branched trees.

3 **SILVER AND BOLD**
A bunch of red rose hips seems to explode from the warm gray patina of a tarnished pewter pitcher.

To: Margaret
From: Katherine

To: Mom
From: Charlie

Brown Paper Packages

Whether tied up with string, decorated with spice rack treasures, or given fanciful flourishes of a more unusual kind, humble brown kraft paper is an inexpensive—yet ideal—canvas for holiday packages. Using the same base paper decked out countless ways keeps the look under the tree simple and cohesive. Get ready to wrap it up!

UNCOMMON OBJECTS

Think beyond traditional adornments for packages and look to the pantry, junk drawer, and ornament bin for bits and pieces to gussy up gifts in unique ways. Reuse old beads, brooches, a stray earring, or broken necklace. Consider the potential in cheap flea market finds to embellish gifts—the options are endless.

NATURAL ELEMENTS

For the gardener, nature-lover, or on hostess gifts, consider organic embellishments such as greenery, woodsy herbs, or winter berries. These lose their fresh luster quickly, so they're best used on presents that will be opened soon after they are wrapped.

To: Sara

CHRISTMAS • MERRY

TIED UP WITH STRING

Twine, string, and ribbon can be used in clever ways to create an
assortment of eye-catching presents. Select materials in gradations
of the same color for a monochromatic look—or choose colors that
suit your decor—then weave, wrap, and secure using glue or tape.

String Embroidery

Personalize gifts for friends and loved ones with a simple monogram or meaningful symbol.

1 Make a dot in the center of the package for reference. Draw your design with a pencil, erasing as necessary until you get it just right. If creating a monogram, it helps to draw the center initial first for balance.

2 Before you begin gluing, trace your design with string, and cut it into appropriate lengths. Working inch by inch, trace each letter with a line of glue, quickly and carefully pressing the string into place as you go. When finished, add further embellishments to the package as desired.

Homespun Holiday

There is something magical about coming home for the holidays. Familiar sights, smells, rooms, and decorations collide to make the sort of big impressions that form enduring memories.

Greenery and plant nursery finds mix with ribbon and burlap in this simple but stunning display.

Garden Greetings

1 GRAND STAND
A utilitarian divided stand takes center stage with a welcoming display of potted plants.

2 DOUBLE DUTY
This enamelware pan-turned-container-garden would make a great gift for anyone with a green thumb—especially with tools tucked in.

3 GARDEN GOODS
A painted wagon serves as a mobile station for cuttings that will be woven into holiday arrangements and newly potted poinsettias and pansies that are sure to brighten rooms.

Forest and Field

1 SOUTHERN STAPLES
In the foyer, the bottom newel post of the garland-strung stair banister is decorated with dried okra pods, cotton bolls, evergreen boughs, and berries tied with a pair of burlap bows, evoking a cozy, down-home mood.

2 STYLISH TABLES
A long console table in the hall shimmers with a scattering of metallic ornaments and flickering candlelight, highlighting the architectural beauty of a trio of amaryllis in full bloom. Unshelled walnuts act as mulch in the tulip-inspired concrete pots.

{1}

{1}

"Christmas is a season for kindling the fire, for hospitality in the hall, the genial flame of charity in the heart."

—WASHINGTON IRVING

{2}

{2}

{1}

Natural Noel

1 SETTING THE SCENE
Consider every surface an opportunity for creative display. A red-striped pillow pops against a creamy slipcovered chair and provides comfort by the fire. On top of an antique wooden trunk now used as a coffee table, a cement bowl with a pinched piecrust lip showcases a bumper crop of tiny Lady apples and plump pomegranates. Vintage wicker-covered wine jugs add further interest.

2 MANTEL MAGIC
Gather an array of objects in varying heights to create an asymmetrical vignette atop the mantel. Here, a veritable forest of trees designed from different materials—muslin, burlap, resin, and rope—serves as the foundation of the display. Wrapped presents, multiple votives, and red ornaments are the fillers that complete the look.

3 NOSTALGIC TOUCHES
Vintage flour sack towels are reincarnated as stockings, each embellished with an antique key and stuffed with Christmas-morning surprises.

{3}

Trim the Tree

1 'TIS A GIFT
Look outside the ornament box for unique trimmings for the tree. Use wire hooks to hang pretty seed packets from the tree's branches. Invite holidays guests to select their favorite to take home.

2 TINSEL WITH TEXTURE
Inexpensive burlap-and-wire bird ornaments fit the agrarian theme perfectly, especially when hung with a variety of seed packets, twine balls, and miniature garden tool ornaments.

3 PRETTY PACKAGES
Save scraps of wrapping paper (or any pretty paper) and ribbon all year long, and then use the remnants in creative ways. Sticking to a theme of cream, red, brown, and silvery sage makes the gifts under the tree as much a part of the decor as the tree itself. Consider them the shoes for the outfit.

Pick a color palette for your holiday decor and repeat it for a cohesive look. Layer those colors with different textures in multiple ways for interest.

"Christmas waves a magic
wand over this world, and
behold, everything is softer
and more beautiful."

— NORMAN VINCENT PEALE

Sweet and Simple

1 EVERYDAY OBJECTS
Favorite things dressed up for the holidays turn out to be the best-loved decorations. Make the holiday wreath even more special by embellishing it with family heirlooms or collections. Though unconventional, antique silver flatware proves to be a perfectly beautiful adornment.

2 SNOW BOLLS
Cotton bolls set a snowy scene—Southern style. Nestle the snow-white plants among boxwood clippings for a homespun touch.

3 NATURAL CHARM
Make your own nature-inspired napkin rings by spray-painting cedar roses (the opened cones of the deodar cedar tree) silver and gluing them to a wide ribbon. Slip in a sprig of greenery for a special flourish.

An enchanted succulent forest dusted with snow is a contemporary center-piece on this round table, perfect for intimate gatherings. A simple flocked wreath attached to a picture window anchors the view beyond. Its shape echoes the circular arrangement.

Tabletop Winterlands

Turn to a frosty palette of pearl white, shades of green, dusty gray, and silver to create soothing wintry arrangements for the center of the table or sideboard.

{2}

Succulent Tray

1 SHADES OF GREEN

Multiple varieties of succulents, purchased in seedling pots, were planted in a gravel-lined zinc tray filled with sanded potting mix. A dusting of artificial snow camouflages the soil and just kisses the leaves, for a snowy landscape effect. Rocks from the yard painted silver serve as shimmering tiny boulders, while flickering votives make the scene sparkle. Placed in a sunny spot and given a weekly misting of water, this living arrangement will thrive long past the holidays.

2 SNOWY SETTING

The organic free-form rims and muted tones of the earthenware plates mixed with the clean lines of the stemware are modern, but together create a table that is warm and inviting. Ornaments become place card holders when name tags are tied on with ribbon. Another option is to pen guests' names directly on the ornaments so that they may take them home as favors to remember the evening.

Woodland
Marvels

1 DAINTY DISPLAY
Unique accents such as this herd of tiny glass reindeer vases have lots of impact when used in multiples. Slices of birch log serve as pedestals for the herd. The log rounds could also be used as trivets to protect the holiday table from hot foods.

2 FLORA AND FAUNA
The twisting lit branches of a lightly flocked artificial tree are the backdrop for this woodsy arrangement and provide height and texture. A large glass canister with a smaller water-filled vase inside is lined with skinny birch logs cut to fit. Like a rustic fence, it contains the bountiful garden of fresh-cut blooms, including hydrangeas, lilies, tulips, and tropical portea mixed with seeded eucalyptus and fuzzy lamb's ears.

{1}

Bloom

1 PAIL OF POSIES
The weathered patina of this galvanized pail appears frost-covered, a fitting look for its contents: snowball-tight blossoms of ranunculus and fragrant lilies.

2 LOW AND LIGHT
This low, lush composition relies on moss-covered florist foam in a shallow pan to support an array of lacy blossoms in muted green, cream, and white.

3 NEW USES
A zinc beverage carrier becomes a portable bouquet of tulips, ranunculus, and narcissus. A gray, bentwood snowflake is a reminder of the season.

{3}

"One touch of nature makes the whole world kin."

—WILLIAM SHAKESPEARE

{2}

Twinkling Terrarium

1 GLASS MENAGERIE

Outside (weather permitting) or indoors, lanterns, apothecary jars, and tiny conservatories can be turned into miniature terrariums by using a variety of plants and objects to create whimsical worlds. Here, outdoors, the magic under glass is carried over to the tabletop for added interest.

2 LUSH LANDSCAPES

Select miniature plant specimens and be sure to start with a bed of gravel for good drainage. Instead of watering the arrangement, plant it in a layer of damp (not wet) soil mixed with horticultural charcoal. Once closed, the humidity level will keep the plants hydrated, but an occasional misting of water may be required from time to time. Moisture-loving plants like fern, moss, peperomia, and fittonia are some of the best choices. Open the terrarium every few weeks to allow it to air out a bit and release built-up condensation. As the year progresses, change out holiday ornaments for other seasonal baubles.

Yule Walls

Think beyond the tree and mantel and add decorative holiday flourishes in unexpected places.

Lit Canvas

1 When space is at a premium or you simply want to take your holiday decorating up a notch, paint a seasonal message on canvas and light it up for all your guests to see. Here, "joy" makes a bold statement in red and is a fitting sentiment hung above a candy-filled tablescape sure to bring smiles to lucky guests.

2 Puncture artwork at regular intervals with a craft knife, and insert twinkling lights through the back. Battery-powered strands allow you to hang your master-piece anywhere.

Jolly Shelves

It's time for the elf to find a new home. Here, one bookshelf decked out two different ways shows the versatility of using an often overlooked spot for holiday decorating.

1 HEART MELTER

No snow? No problem! Make a snowman inside this year. This little man won't melt … but hearts will. Three plastic foam spheres in varying sizes, coated with foam adhesive and sprinkled with artificial snow, look like the real deal. Shelves are placed to divide each sphere. The snowman comes to life with button eyes and mouth, a quintessential carrot nose, and striped scarf. Twigs become arms, and a top hat completes the look. Artificial snow drifts mound on the shelves around ornament snowballs. Frosty will stay toasty this year!

2 CHEERY NOOK

A beloved china collection becomes a graphic display in red and white. Cake stands placed on each shelf and topped with carefully arranged pomegranates form a scarlet "tree" in an otherwise dark corner. More pieces—teacups, pitchers, and mugs—serve as vases for ranunculus and red berries to create a holiday vignette that would be perfect in a dining room or kitchen.

{1}

Wall Tree

1 ORGANIC ACCENTS
An earthy stone wall backdrop provides the proper setting for ornaments crafted from wood and shimmering metallics. Snowflakes predominate, but other woodland finds such as acorns, pine cones, and owls are woven into the mix.

2 FLAT FLOURISH
This one-dimensional wonder is a great eco-alternative to the usual evergreen. It's collapsible, too, making it an ideal choice when space is at a premium. Organic materials and shapes—from the twig starburst topper all the way down to the table beneath—provide a cohesive design. Grapevine balls and a few branches of greenery enhance the look.

{1}

Savor

FROM APPETIZERS TO DESSERTS, WE PRESENT
THE SEASON'S MUST-HAVE RECIPES.

Get the Party Started

The holidays only roll around once a year, so it's time to fill up those glasses with some winter-inspired drinks and put the party food out on the counter. Here are Christmas-inspired variations on some classic cocktails and delicious party food that will keep your guests coming back year after year.

Cranberry Tea-ini

Makes: 2 servings
Hands-On Time: 5 min. Total Time: 5 min.

To make frozen sugared cranberries, dip frozen berries in water, and roll in granulated sugar; refreeze.

- ½ cup fresh or frozen cranberries, thawed
- 2 Tbsp. superfine sugar
- 1 cup ice cubes
- ½ cup sweet tea-flavored vodka
- ¼ cup cranberry juice
- 2 Tbsp. dry vermouth
  Garnishes: 4 frozen sugared cranberries, 2 lemon zest twists

Place ½ cup cranberries and superfine sugar in a cocktail shaker. Muddle cranberries against sides of shaker to release flavors; add ice, vodka, cranberry juice, and vermouth. Cover with lid, and shake vigorously until thoroughly chilled (about 30 seconds). Strain into 2 chilled martini glasses. Serve immediately.

Blueberry-Lime Mojitos

Makes: 4 servings
Hands-On Time: 5 min. Total Time: 5 min.

- 1 lime, cut into 8 wedges
- 8 fresh mint sprigs
- 2 cups crushed ice
- 2 cups wild blueberry sorbet
- 1 cup light rum
- 1 (12-oz.) bottle sparkling lime-flavored juice beverage
  Garnishes: fresh mint sprigs, lime wedges

Muddle 2 lime wedges and 2 mint sprigs against sides of 4 highball glasses to release flavors. Fill each glass with ½ cup ice and ½ cup sorbet. Pour ¼ cup rum and 3 oz. juice beverage over sorbet in each glass. Gently stir, if desired. Serve immediately.

Winter Sangria

Makes: 12 cups
Hands-On Time: 10 min.
Total Time: 8 hours, 10 min.

Clementines bring a fresh seasonal flavor to this popular wine punch.

- ½ cup orange liqueur
- 2 large, firm, ripe red Anjou or Bartlett pears, cored and chopped
- 2 clementines, peeled and sectioned
- 2 kiwifruit, peeled and chopped
- 1 (750-milliliter) bottle sparkling red wine
- 4 cups sparkling orange drink
- ½ cup fresh lemon juice
- 1 lemon, sliced
- 1 clementine, sliced
  Ice cubes

1. Combine liqueur, chopped pears, clementine sections, and kiwifruit in a large glass bowl or gallon-size zip-top plastic freezer bag. Cover or seal, and chill 8 hours.
2. Combine wine, orange drink, lemon juice, lemon slices, clementine slices, and soaked fruit in a large pitcher or punch bowl. Serve over ice.

NOTE: We tested with Cointreau, Orangina, and Rosa di Rosa sparkling red wine.

QUICK & EASY
Ruby Red Negroni

Makes: 6 servings
Hands-On Time: 7 min. Total Time: 7 min.

Our twist on the classic Negroni features fresh ruby red grapefruit juice for a festive drink to ring in the holidays.

- 2 cups fresh red grapefruit juice (3 large grapefruit)
- 1 cup gin
- 1 cup Campari
- 1 cup sweet vermouth
  Crushed ice
- 1½ cups club soda
  Garnish: fresh orange slices

1. Stir together first 4 ingredients in a pitcher. Cover and chill.
2. Fill 6 double old-fashioned glasses with crushed ice. Divide juice mixture evenly among glasses. Top each serving with ¼ cup club soda, and stir gently. Serve immediately.

Cranberry-Chutney Cheese Ball

Makes: 8 to 10 appetizer servings
Hands-On Time: 10 min. Total Time: 3 hours, 20 min.

If you can make this cheese ball ahead of time, the flavor blend is fantastic.

- 1 (8-oz.) package cream cheese, softened
- 1 (8-oz.) block extra-sharp white Cheddar cheese, shredded
- 1/2 cup mango chutney
- 1/2 tsp. curry powder
- 1/8 tsp. ground red pepper
- 1 cup sweetened dried cranberries
- 1/3 cup chopped green onions
- 1 cup chopped pistachios
  Flatbread crackers

1. Beat cream cheese at medium speed with an electric mixer in a large bowl until smooth. Reduce speed to low; add Cheddar cheese, and beat until well blended.
2. Chop any large pieces of chutney. Add chutney, curry powder, and red pepper to cream cheese mixture, beating at low speed just until blended. Stir in cranberries and green onions.
3. Shape mixture into a ball; wrap in plastic wrap, and chill 3 to 24 hours.
4. Roll cheese ball in chopped pistachios. Let stand 10 minutes before serving. Serve with crackers.

NOTE: We tested with Cracker Barrel Extra-Sharp Cheddar Cheese and Craisins.

Cheese Biscuit Barbecue Bites

Makes: 45 servings
Hands-On Time: 30 min. Total Time: 50 min.

Grits add texture and a unique twist to these cheesy buttermilk biscuits. Paired with barbecued pork, these sliders are sure to be an instant hit at your holiday party.

- 2 cups self-rising flour
- 2/3 cup uncooked quick-cooking grits
- 1/4 tsp. freshly ground black pepper
- 1/2 cup cold butter, cut into pieces
- 4 oz. sharp Cheddar cheese, shredded
- 2 Tbsp. finely chopped green onions
- 3/4 cup buttermilk
- 2 Tbsp. butter, melted
- 3/4 lb. shredded barbecued pork without sauce, warmed
- 1/2 cup barbecue sauce

1. Preheat oven to 425°. Stir together first 3 ingredients in a large bowl; cut 1/2 cup butter into flour mixture with a pastry blender or fork until mixture resembles small peas and dough is crumbly. Stir in cheese and green onions. Add buttermilk, stirring just until dry ingredients are moistened.
2. Turn dough out onto a lightly floured surface, and knead lightly 3 or 4 times. Pat or roll dough to 1/2-inch thickness; cut with a 1 1/2-inch round cutter, and place on a lightly greased baking sheet. Brush tops of biscuits with 2 Tbsp. melted butter.
3. Bake at 425° for 10 minutes or until golden brown.
4. Combine pork and barbecue sauce in small bowl. Split biscuits; fill with pork mixture before serving.

QUICK & EASY
Creamy Blue Cheese–and–Spicy Plum Mini Tarts

Makes: 15 servings
Hands-On Time: 7 min. Total Time: 13 min.

Sure to be a crowd-pleaser, these mini tarts feature soft blue cheese, sweet-and-spicy plum preserves, and candied walnuts. Prepackaged frozen mini-phyllo shells make assembling quick and simple.

- 2 Tbsp. plum preserves
- 1 Tbsp. ruby port
- 1/4 tsp. freshly ground black pepper
- 3 oz. Cambozola or other soft blue cheese
- 1 (2.1-oz.) package frozen mini-phyllo pastry shells, thawed
- 2 Tbsp. chopped candied walnuts

1. Preheat oven to 375°. Stir together first 3 ingredients in a small bowl. Cut cheese into 15 cubes; place 1 cube into each phyllo shell. Top each cheese cube with about 1/2 teaspoonful preserves mixture.
2. Place shells on a baking sheet. Bake at 375° for 6 minutes. Sprinkle with candied walnuts.

Turkey-Artichoke Cornucopias

Makes: 18 servings
Hands-On Time: 45 min. Total Time: 1 hour, 21 min.

A cornucopia, or "horn of plenty," is a symbol of abundance and overflowing gifts. These bite-size treats are perfect at every holiday occasion. Leftover chicken salad works equally well in these pastries. See the directions below to make your own cream horn molds using heavy-duty aluminum foil.

2	**cups finely chopped roasted turkey**
1/2	**cup drained and finely chopped marinated artichoke hearts**
1/2	**cup mayonnaise**
1/3	**cup finely shredded Parmesan cheese**
2	**Tbsp. finely chopped green onions**
1/4	**tsp. table salt**
	Cream horn molds
	Vegetable cooking spray
1/2	**(17.3-oz) package frozen puff pastry sheets, thawed**
1	**large egg**
	Coarse or flaky sea salt

1. Stir together first 6 ingredients in a medium bowl; cover and chill at least 1 hour.

2. Preheat oven to 375°. Coat cream horn molds with cooking spray.

3. Unfold pastry sheet on a lightly floured surface; gently smooth out lines with a rolling pin. Cut dough crosswise into 18 (1/2-inch) strips using a pizza cutter. (Do not separate strips.) Whisk together egg and 1 Tbsp. water; brush tops of strips with egg mixture.

4. Starting at tip end of cream horn molds, wrap 1 strip of pastry, egg side out, about halfway up each mold, overlapping slightly and forming a cornucopia. (Do not stretch pastry.) Repeat procedure with remaining molds and pastry strips. If working in batches, chill remaining pastry strips until ready to use. Place cream horn molds 2 inches apart on a lightly greased baking sheet, with ends of pastry strips facing down. Brush with egg mixture.

5. Bake at 375° for 18 to 20 minutes or until lightly browned. Transfer to wire rack; cool 5 minutes. Remove molds; let pastries cool completely (about 20 minutes).

6. Spoon turkey salad into a large zip-top plastic bag. Snip 1 corner of bag to make a hole about 3/4-inch in diameter. Gently pipe turkey salad into each pastry horn.

NOTE: You can order cream horn molds from Amazon.com or King Arthur Flour, or purchase at a local kitchen store. You can also make your own using the easy instructions below. If you have two sets of six, it will cut baking time in half.

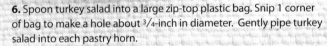

To make your own cream horn molds:

Cut 18 (6- x 4-inch) strips of heavy-duty aluminum foil. Roll up 1 foil strip diagonally to form a cone with a 1 1/2-inch diameter opening. Repeat procedure with remaining strips of foil. Crumple additional foil to place inside cones to make them more sturdy. (The outside of foil molds does not have to remain smooth.)

Comforting Soups & Stews

Nothing says Christmas quite like the familiar aroma of freshly made comfort foods emanating from your kitchen. Stay warm this winter with these savory soups and stews. These holiday favorites are sure to please friends and family, and will keep them coming back for more.

Pumpkin Soup with Red Pepper Relish

Makes: 10 cups
Hands-On Time: 24 min. Total Time: 40 min.

Top off this pretty soup with toasted pumpkin seeds.

- 3 Tbsp. butter
- 5 carrots, chopped
- 1 large sweet onion, chopped
- 2 garlic cloves, minced
- 5 cups chicken broth
- ¾ tsp. table salt
- ½ tsp. ground cumin
- ¼ tsp. freshly ground black pepper
- 2 (15-oz.) cans pumpkin
- ¼ cup whipping cream
  Red Pepper Relish

1. Melt butter in a large Dutch oven over medium heat. Sauté carrots, onion, and garlic 5 to 6 minutes or until tender. Add chicken broth, salt, cumin, black pepper, and pumpkin. Bring to a boil; reduce heat to medium-low, and simmer 10 minutes, stirring occasionally. Cool 10 minutes.
2. Process pumpkin mixture, in batches, in a blender until smooth, stopping to scrape down sides as needed. Return mixture to Dutch oven; stir in whipping cream. Cook just until thoroughly heated.
3. Ladle soup into bowls, and top with Red Pepper Relish before serving.

Red Pepper Relish

Makes: 1 cup
Hands-On Time: 5 min. Total Time: 5 min.

- 1 (12-oz.) jar roasted red bell peppers, drained and finely chopped
- 2 Tbsp. chopped fresh cilantro
- 1 Tbsp. olive oil
- 1 tsp. fresh lime juice
- ¼ tsp. table salt
- ¼ tsp. smoked paprika

Stir together all ingredients.

Ham-and-Corn Chowder

Makes: 8 servings
Hands-On Time: 51 min. Total Time: 51 min.

This is a nice way to use up leftover holiday ham.

- 1½ cups finely chopped ham
- 1 Tbsp. olive oil
- 2 (16-oz.) packages frozen baby gold and white corn, thawed and divided
- 1 small onion, chopped
- 1 small red bell pepper, chopped
- 2 celery ribs, chopped
- 2 garlic cloves, minced
- 2 Tbsp. all-purpose flour
- 1 lb. unpeeled red potatoes, cut into ½-inch cubes
- 2 cups milk, divided
- 2 tsp. thyme leaves
- 1 (14.5-oz.) can chicken broth
- 1 cup heavy cream
- 1 cup (4-oz.) shredded sharp Cheddar cheese
- ½ tsp. freshly ground black pepper
- ½ tsp. table salt

1. Sauté ham in hot oil in a Dutch oven over medium heat until lightly browned. Remove ham from Dutch oven using a slotted spoon; reserve drippings. Sauté 1 package corn and next 4 ingredients in hot drippings 5 minutes or until tender.
2. Sprinkle flour over vegetables; cook, stirring constantly, 1 minute. Add potatoes, 1 cup milk, thyme, and broth. Bring to a boil; reduce heat, and simmer 15 minutes or until potatoes are almost tender, stirring occasionally.
3. Process remaining 1 package corn and remaining 1 cup milk in a blender; stir into potato mixture. Simmer 15 minutes, stirring occasionally. Return ham to soup; stir in cream and remaining ingredients. Cook 2 minutes or until cheese melts.

Braised Beef-and-Mushroom Stew

Makes: 10 servings
Hands-On Time: 30 min. Total Time: 2 hours, 33 min.

For an even heartier meal, serve this stew over mashed potatoes or creamy polenta.

- 3 lb. beef stew meat
- 1/2 tsp. table salt
- 3/4 tsp. freshly ground black pepper, divided
- 1/2 cup all-purpose flour
- 1/4 cup butter, divided
- 1/4 cup olive oil
- 3 garlic cloves, minced
- 3 (8-oz.) packages fresh mushrooms, quartered
- 1 large onion, cut into wedges
- 1 cup dry red wine
- 4 cups beef broth
- 1 Tbsp. tomato paste
- 2 tsp. fresh thyme leaves
- 1 tsp. chopped fresh rosemary
- 4 large carrots, peeled and cut into 1-inch pieces (3 cups)
- 1 Tbsp. all-purpose flour
  Garnish: fresh thyme or rosemary sprigs

1. Sprinkle beef with salt and 1/2 tsp. black pepper. Place 1/2 cup flour in a shallow dish. Dredge beef in flour; shake off excess.

2. Heat 1 Tbsp. butter and 2 Tbsp. oil in a large Dutch oven over medium-high heat until butter is melted. Add half of beef to pan. Cook 8 to 10 minutes or until beef is browned on all sides. Remove beef from pan. Repeat procedure with 1 Tbsp. butter, remaining 2 Tbsp. oil, and remaining beef.

3. Heat remaining 2 Tbsp. butter in pan until butter is melted. Add garlic, mushrooms, and onion. Cook over medium-high heat 22 minutes or until mushrooms are browned, stirring occasionally. Stir in red wine. Bring to a boil; cook, uncovered, 10 minutes or until wine is reduced by half. Return beef to pan; add beef broth and tomato paste. Bring to a boil; cover, reduce heat, and simmer 1 hour or until beef is tender.

4. Add thyme and next 2 ingredients. Cover and cook over medium heat 30 minutes or until carrots are tender.

5. Combine 1 Tbsp. flour and 1/4 cup cold water, stirring until blended and smooth. Gradually stir flour mixture and remaining 1/4 tsp. black pepper into stew. Cook, uncovered, 10 minutes or until thickened, stirring occasionally.

Oyster-and-Wild Rice Bisque

Makes: 9 cups
Hands-On Time: 35 min. Total Time: 45 min.

Wild rice replaces potatoes in this classic holiday soup.

- ¹/₂ cup uncooked wild rice
- 4 bacon slices
- 2 Tbsp. butter or margarine
- 1¹/₂ cups chopped onion
- ¹/₂ cup finely chopped celery
- 3 garlic cloves, minced
- ¹/₄ cup dry white wine
- 1 bay leaf
- 3 Tbsp. all-purpose flour
- 2 cups milk
- 1¹/₂ cups whipping cream
- 2 pt. fresh oysters, undrained
- 1 tsp. table salt
- ¹/₈ tsp. ground red pepper

1. Cook wild rice according to package directions; drain.
2. Cook bacon in a Dutch oven over medium heat 6 minutes or until crisp; remove bacon, and drain on paper towels, reserving 1 Tbsp. drippings in pan. Crumble bacon.
3. Melt butter with reserved hot drippings in Dutch oven over medium heat; add onion and celery, and sauté 5 minutes or until tender. Add garlic; sauté 1 minute. Add wine and bay leaf; cook 1 minute. Stir together flour, milk, and whipping cream until smooth; add to mixture in Dutch oven. Bring to a boil; reduce heat, and simmer, stirring often, over medium heat 7 to 8 minutes or until slightly thickened. Stir in oysters, oyster liquor, salt, ground red pepper, and cooked rice. Cook 5 minutes or just until edges of oysters begin to curl. Ladle soup into bowls, and sprinkle with crumbled bacon.

Curried Parsnip Bisque

Makes: 10 cups
Hands-On Time: 15 min. Total Time: 1 hour, 30 min.

Roasted parsnips are the base of this creamy soup spiked with curry powder. For an elegant presentation, drizzle parsley oil over each serving.

- 3 lb. parsnips
- 3 Tbsp. olive oil, divided
- 3 oz. thinly sliced pancetta
- 1 medium leek, sliced (2 cups)
- ³/₄ cup chopped onion
- ³/₄ cup chopped celery
- 1 Tbsp. curry powder
- ¹/₂ tsp. table salt
- ¹/₂ tsp. freshly ground black pepper
- 5 cups chicken broth, divided
- 1¹/₂ cups heavy cream
  Garnish: fresh parsley

1. Preheat oven to 450°. Peel parsnips, and cut into 1-inch pieces. Place in a roasting pan. Drizzle with 1 Tbsp. oil, tossing to coat.
2. Bake at 450° for 30 to 35 minutes or just until tender.
3. Separate pancetta into slices. Cook pancetta, in batches, in a Dutch oven over medium-high heat 3 to 4 minutes or until crisp; remove pancetta, and drain on paper towels.
4. Add remaining 2 Tbsp. oil to Dutch oven. Sauté leek, onion, and celery in hot oil 5 to 6 minutes or until tender. Stir in curry powder, salt, and black pepper; cook 1 minute or until fragrant. Add parsnips and 4 cups chicken broth; bring to a boil. Reduce heat to medium, and simmer, uncovered, 35 to 40 minutes or until vegetables are very tender. Cool 10 minutes.
5. Process vegetable mixture, in batches, in a blender until smooth, stopping to scrape down sides as needed. Return mixture to Dutch oven. Stir in heavy cream and remaining 1 cup broth; simmer, uncovered, 5 minutes or until thoroughly heated.
6. To serve, ladle soup into bowls, and top with pancetta.

Top Turkey

Go traditional or get creative with your turkey this holiday season. Here are several recipes that will add some flavor to everyone's favorite holiday main dish. Add a down-South kick to your turkey with a sweet and tangy BBQ sauce, or drop it in the deep fryer for a taste that no one can resist.

Roast Turkey and Brown Gravy

Makes: 10 to 12 servings
Hands-On Time: 25 min. Total Time: 3 hours, 40 min.

One cold, gray Christmas Day in London, my fellow Pan Am flight crew and I entered the hotel in Chelsea where we stayed. Hungry, tired, and a bit dejected about spending another holiday away from home, we were greeted by the smoky aroma of roast turkey wafting into the lobby. That wonderful scent transported me at once to the Cratchit home where I imagined Bob preparing to carve Scrooge's succulent gift. I don't have their recipe, but when my version is roasting, it smells just like my memory of that splendid Christmas bird. I'm sure Tiny Tim would heartily approve. Wrapping the veggies in wet cheesecloth adds moisture and flavor from the inside out, so the turkey is flavorful and juicy even though you don't baste it. —Julie Christopher

TURKEY:

- 1 (12- to 13-lb.) fresh or frozen natural turkey, thawed
- 2 cups coarsely chopped onion, divided
- 2 cups coarsely chopped celery, divided
- 1 tsp. dried Italian seasoning
- 6 whole black peppercorns
- 2 tsp. table salt, divided
    Vegetable cooking spray
- ³/₄ tsp. freshly ground black pepper, divided
- 1¼ tsp. garlic powder, divided
    Cheesecloth
- 3 Tbsp. canola oil

BROWN GRAVY:

- Pan drippings from Roast Turkey
- ¹/₃ cup all-purpose flour

1. Preheat oven to 325° with rack in lower third of oven. Remove giblets and neck from turkey. Rinse giblets and place in a 3- to 4-qt. saucepan. Add 1 cup each onion and celery, next 2 ingredients, 1 tsp. salt, and ¹/₂ qt. water. Bring to a boil over high heat. Reduce heat to low; partially cover, and simmer 1¹/₂ hours. Strain broth to measure 1 qt., adding water if necessary. Discard solids.
2. While broth simmers, toss together remaining onion and celery in a bowl. Rinse turkey, and pat dry with paper towels. Spray broiler pan and both sides of rack with cooking spray. Sprinkle body and neck cavities of turkey with ¹/₂ tsp. salt and ¹/₄ tsp. pepper. Sprinkle ¹/₄ tsp. garlic powder in body cavity.
3. Wrap 1¹/₂ cups onion mixture in 2 layers of cheesecloth. Saturate cheesecloth packet with water; squeeze out excess moisture, and place in body cavity. Repeat procedure with remaining ¹/₂ cup onion mixture; place in neck cavity. Cover packet with neck skin, folding wing tips under to secure. Tie legs together with kitchen string.
4. Place turkey, breast side up, on prepared broiler pan. Sprinkle bird with ¹/₂ tsp. salt, remaining ¹/₂ tsp. pepper, and remaining 1 tsp. garlic powder, and rub evenly over skin. Brush bird with canola oil. Bake at 325° for 15 minutes per pound or until a meat thermometer inserted in thigh registers 180° and drumstick is soft to touch and leg moves easily (3 to 3¹/₄ hours).
5. Remove turkey from pan, and place on a platter, reserving drippings in pan. Cover turkey with foil, and let rest 45 minutes before carving.
6. Meanwhile, prepare gravy, using a rubber spatula to scrape drippings, including all fat and dark brown bits, into a 2-cup liquid measuring cup. (Do not use any bitter charred bits.) Allow fat to rise to top of drippings. Pour ¹/₃ cup fat into a 3-qt. saucepan. Carefully drain remaining fat, reserving all brown drippings (about 1¹/₄ cups). Whisk flour into fat in saucepan until smooth. Whisk in brown drippings. Cook, whisking constantly, over medium-high heat until bubbly. Whisk in strained broth. Bring to a boil, whisking constantly; reduce heat to medium. Cook, uncovered, 10 minutes or until desired consistency, stirring often. (Gravy will thicken as it cools.)
7. Remove and discard packets from turkey. Carve each side of turkey breast from turkey in one piece. Cut breast halves crosswise into ¹/₄-inch slices. Carve remaining turkey. Serve with gravy.

MAKE AHEAD: Cook, strain, and chill broth a day ahead. Prepare turkey for baking (do not brush with oil), and place on a jelly-roll pan. Refrigerate, uncovered, overnight. Transfer turkey to prepared broiler pan. Brush bird with oil, and bake as directed. (Refrigerating the bird uncovered produces an extra crispy skin.)

Butterflied and Barbecued Turkey

Makes: 10 to 12 servings
Hands-On Time: 3 hours, 3 min.
Total Time: 3 hours, 3 min., plus 8 hours for chilling

A turkey cooked low and slow on direct heat will result in a smoky-flavored, tender, succulent bird without having to use a smoker. Butter-flying the turkey allows the skin to brown and the meat to cook quicker.

- 1 (10- to 12-lb.) whole fresh or frozen turkey, thawed
- 1½ Tbsp. olive oil
- 1½ tsp. table salt
- ¾ tsp. garlic powder
- ¾ tsp. dried Italian seasoning
- ¾ tsp. paprika
- ½ tsp. chili powder
- ½ tsp. ground red pepper
- ½ tsp. freshly ground black pepper
  Sweet-and-Tangy Barbecue Sauce, divided
  Vegetable cooking spray

1. Remove giblets and neck, and rinse turkey with cold water. Drain cavity well; pat dry with paper towels.

2. Cut turkey, using kitchen shears, along both sides of backbone, separating backbone from the turkey. Remove and discard backbone. Press turkey until flattened, and brush entire bird with oil.

3. Combine salt and next 6 ingredients; rub spice mixture evenly on turkey skin and underside. Place turkey in a large shallow dish, large oven bag, or 2-gal. zip-top plastic bag. Cover or seal, and chill in refrigerator 8 to 24 hours.

4. Reserve 1 cup Sweet-and-Tangy Barbecue Sauce to serve with cooked turkey. Light one side of grill, heating to 400° to 500° (high) heat; leave other side unlit. Coat unlit side with cooking spray. Shield wing tips and legs with aluminum foil to prevent excessive browning. Place turkey, skin side up, over unlit side, and grill, covered with grill lid, 2 to 3 hours or until a meat thermometer inserted into thickest portion of thigh registers 170°, basting with remaining Sweet-and-Tangy Barbecue Sauce during last 30 minutes of cooking.

5. Remove turkey from grill to a large shallow dish. Cover with foil, and let stand 15 minutes before carving. Serve with reserved Sweet-and-Tangy Barbecue Sauce.

Sweet-and-Tangy Barbecue Sauce

Makes: 3 cups
Hands-On Time: 11 min. Total Time: 58 min.

- 1 (14.5-oz.) can chicken broth
- 1¾ cups white wine vinegar
- 1¾ cups ketchup
- ½ cup finely chopped onion
- ⅓ cup orange marmalade
- ¼ cup firmly packed brown sugar
- 2½ Tbsp. ancho chile powder
- 2 Tbsp. garlic salt
- 2 tsp. freshly ground pepper

Combine all ingredients in a large saucepan; bring to a boil. Reduce heat, and simmer, stirring often, 45 minutes or until thickened.

Sorghum-Glazed Turkey Breast

Makes: 10 servings
Hands-On Time: 2 hours, 15 min. Total Time: 12 hours, 25 min.

This roast turkey stays moist and succulent as a result of overnight brining. The frequent basting during cooking gives awesome bronzed results at the table.

- 1½ cups sorghum syrup, divided
- ½ cup firmly packed dark brown sugar
- ⅓ cup kosher salt
- 1 Tbsp. whole peppercorns
- 5 bay leaves
- 2 (6-inch) fresh rosemary sprigs
- 1 qt. cold water
- 1 (6- to 7-lb.) bone-in, skin-on fresh turkey breast*
- 2 gal. food-safe container
- ⅓ cup butter, melted and divided
- 1 cup apple cider
- Garnishes: fresh rosemary sprigs, Lady apples, cranberries

1. Combine 1 cup sorghum syrup, next 5 ingredients, and 1 qt. water in a Dutch oven; bring to a boil over medium heat, stirring until sugar and salt dissolve. Remove from heat; stir in 1 qt. cold water. Cool completely.

2. Place turkey, breast side down, in 2-gal. food-safe container. Gradually add brine. Cover and chill 8 hours or overnight, turning twice.

3. Remove turkey from brine, discarding liquid. Rinse turkey, and pat dry with paper towels.

4. Preheat oven to 325°. Place turkey, breast side up, on a rack in an aluminum foil-lined roasting pan. Brush turkey with half of melted butter. Loosely cover turkey with aluminum foil. Bake at 325° for 1 hour.

5. Meanwhile, cook apple cider in a small saucepan over medium-high heat 15 to 20 minutes or until cider is reduced by half. Stir in remaining ½ cup sorghum and remaining melted butter. Uncover turkey; heavily baste turkey with cider mixture. Bake at 325° for 1 hour and 45 minutes or until a meat thermometer registers 170°, basting with cider mixture every 15 minutes, and shielding with aluminum foil during last 30 minutes of baking. Remove from oven; cover loosely with aluminum foil. Let stand 10 minutes. Transfer turkey to a serving platter.

*Frozen turkey breast, thawed, may be substituted.

Herb and Garlic Deep-Fried Turkey

Makes: 8 servings
Hands-On Time: 10 min. Total Time: 2 hours, 15 min.

A fresh turkey is better to use for frying, but if using a frozen turkey, make sure it is completely thawed before cooking. It is essential to thoroughly drain any turkey before frying to prevent the oil from popping.

- Peanut oil (about 3 gal.)
- 1 (12- to 14-lb.) whole fresh turkey
- 2 Tbsp. kosher salt
- 2 tsp. dried thyme
- 2 tsp. dried rosemary
- 2 tsp. ground sage
- 2 tsp. garlic powder
- 1 tsp. freshly ground black pepper

1. Pour oil into a deep propane turkey fryer 10 to 12 inches from top; heat to 350° over a medium-low flame according to manufacturer's instructions (about 45 minutes).

2. Meanwhile, remove giblets and neck from turkey. Place turkey on fryer rod. Drain on paper towels (about 1 hour); pat dry.

3. Stir together salt and next 5 ingredients in a small bowl. Loosen and lift skin from turkey without totally detaching skin; spread one-fourth salt mixture under skin. Carefully replace skin. Sprinkle one-fourth salt mixture inside cavity; rub into cavity. Sprinkle outside of turkey with remaining salt mixture; rub into skin.

4. Carefully lower turkey into hot oil with rod attachment. Fry turkey 2 to 2½ minutes per pound or until a meat thermometer inserted in thigh registers 170°. (Keep oil temperature at 350°.) Remove turkey from oil; drain and let cool slightly before slicing (about 15 minutes).

All the Trimmings

Showcase any of these glorious turkeys in holiday splendor by serving it on a platter slightly larger than the bird and surrounding it with any of these festive garnishes:

POPS OF CITRUS—slices of navel or blood oranges, small tangerines, or kumquats

WINTER'S BOUNTY—small bunches of red or green grapes, muscadines, or Concord grapes

FRAGRANT HERBS—sprigs of sage, rosemary, thyme, or tarragon

A BASE OF GREEN—fig leaves, grapevines, or collard greens

Good
Gravy

Everyone's favorite part of a
home-cooked holiday meal. Serve up
heaping helpings of these variations of
traditional home-style gravies. What could
be better than some gravy with bacon,
mushrooms, eggs, or tomato?

Roasted Tomato-Thyme Gravy

Makes: 4 cups
Hands-On Time: 18 min. Total Time: 25 min.

The tomato paste acts as a thickener in this gravy, reducing the chance of lumps from flour, the traditional thickener.

- 2 cups chopped onion
- 2 Tbsp. olive oil
- 2 garlic cloves, minced
- 3 Tbsp. tomato paste
- 2 cups chicken broth or turkey pan drippings, skimmed of fat
- 1 (14½-oz.) can fire-roasted diced tomatoes
- 2 Tbsp. fresh thyme leaves
- 1 bay leaf
- ½ cup whipping cream
- ¾ tsp. table salt
- ½ tsp. ancho chile powder
- ¼ tsp. freshly ground black pepper
- Garnish: chopped fresh thyme

Sauté onion in hot oil in a medium saucepan over medium heat 3 minutes or until tender. Add garlic; sauté 1 minute. Add tomato paste; cook 2 minutes, stirring often. Gradually whisk in broth. Bring to a boil over medium-high heat, whisking constantly. Add tomatoes, thyme, and bay leaf; reduce heat to low, and simmer, stirring often, 10 minutes or until thoroughly heated. Stir in whipping cream, salt, chile powder, and black pepper; cook 1 minute. Remove and discard bay leaf.

Mushroom Gravy

Makes: 10 to 12 servings
Hands-On Time: 26 min. Total Time: 26 min.

Use any leftover gravy over mashed potatoes, beef roast, or steak.

- 2 Tbsp. butter
- 1 (8-oz.) package sliced baby portobello mushrooms
- ¼ cup dry sherry
- 2 Tbsp. all-purpose flour
- 2 cups vegetable broth
- ½ cup whipping cream
- 2 tsp. chopped fresh thyme
- ½ tsp. table salt
- ½ tsp. freshly ground black pepper

1. Melt butter in a large skillet over medium-high heat. Add mushrooms; sauté 5 to 6 minutes or until tender. Stir in sherry, and cook 1 minute or until liquid almost evaporates. Stir in flour, and cook, stirring constantly, 1 minute. Gradually stir in broth. Bring to a boil; reduce heat, and simmer, stirring constantly, 5 minutes or until slightly thickened.
2. Stir in cream. Simmer 8 minutes, stirring constantly, or until thickened. Remove from heat, and stir in thyme, salt, and black pepper.

Simple Herbed Gravy with Egg

Makes: 4 cups
Hands-On Time: 30 min. Total Time: 30 min.

This gravy pairs well with both your holiday turkey and dressing. Find hard-cooked eggs in the dairy or deli section of your grocery store if you don't have time to cook your own.

- ¼ cup butter
- ½ cup chopped sweet onion
- 2 garlic cloves, minced
- ½ cup all-purpose flour
- 4 cups chicken broth
- 2 Tbsp. chopped fresh parsley
- 2 tsp. chopped fresh thyme
- 1 tsp. chopped fresh rosemary
- ½ tsp. table salt
- ½ tsp. freshly black ground pepper
- 4 hard-cooked eggs, peeled and chopped

Melt butter in a large saucepan over medium heat; add onion, and sauté 4 minutes or until tender. Add garlic; sauté 30 seconds. Stir in flour, and cook, stirring constantly, 1 minute. Gradually whisk in broth, and cook over medium-high heat, stirring constantly, 15 minutes or until thickened. Remove from heat; stir in herbs, salt, pepper, and eggs.

Bacon-Apple Gravy

Makes: 10 to 12 servings
Hands-On Time: 23 min. Total Time: 23 min.

Bacon adds a nice smoky flavor to this cider-based gravy. Make sure to use a cooking apple that will maintain its shape when sautéed, such as a Fuji or Braeburn.

- 4 applewood-smoked bacon slices
- ½ cup chopped onion
- 1 medium Fuji or Braeburn apple, peeled and chopped
- 2 garlic cloves, minced
- 3 Tbsp. all-purpose flour
- 2 cups apple cider
- 1 cup chicken broth
- ½ tsp. table salt
- ½ tsp. freshly ground black pepper
- 1 Tbsp. chopped fresh sage

1. Cook bacon in a large skillet over medium-high heat 6 to 8 minutes or until crisp; remove bacon, and drain on paper towels, reserving 2 Tbsp. drippings in skillet. Crumble bacon.
2. Sauté onion and apple in hot drippings 5 minutes or until tender. Add garlic, and sauté 30 seconds. Stir in flour and cook, stirring constantly, 1 minute. Gradually stir in cider and broth. Bring to a boil; reduce heat, and simmer, stirring constantly, 6 minutes or until slightly thickened. Remove from heat. Stir in salt, black pepper, sage, and reserved bacon.

The Main Event

Feast like a king this Christmas on these delicious main courses. From pork to beef to duck to lamb, there's something for the whole family to enjoy. These traditional main courses are kicked up a notch with savory flavorings that will give it that familiar wintery taste.

Crown Pork Roast with Fig-Fennel Stuffing

Makes: 12 servings
Hands-On Time: 35 min. Total Time: 4 hours, 40 min.

Make your holiday extra-special by serving this herb-rubbed crown roast filled with moist Fig-Fennel Stuffing. For a time-saving measure, have your butcher french the chops and tie the roast in a crown.

- 1 Tbsp. fennel seeds
- 1 Tbsp. coriander seeds
- 1 Tbsp. chopped fresh thyme
- 2 tsp. kosher salt
- 2 tsp. freshly ground pepper
- 2 tsp. lemon zest
- 5 large garlic cloves, minced
- 3 Tbsp. olive oil
- 1 (16-rib) crown pork roast, trimmed and tied (10 to 11 lb.)
  Fig-Fennel Stuffing
- 1 Tbsp. butter
- 1 Tbsp. chopped shallot
- 1 Tbsp. all-purpose flour
- 1/3 cup dry white wine
- 1/4 cup chicken broth
- 1/2 cup whipping cream
- 1/4 tsp. freshly ground black pepper
  Garnishes: fresh thyme sprigs, fresh figs, fresh currants

1. Preheat oven to 350°. Place a small skillet over medium-high heat until hot; add fennel and coriander seeds, and cook, stirring constantly, 1 to 2 minutes or until toasted. Let cool 5 minutes; coarsely crush seeds.
2. Combine crushed fennel and coriander seeds, chopped thyme, and next 4 ingredients in a small bowl. Stir in olive oil until blended. Rub spice mixture evenly over all sides of pork roast. Place roast in a lightly greased roasting pan. Spoon 3 1/2 cups Fig-Fennel Stuffing into center of roast. Cover stuffing with a square of aluminum foil. Cap the end of each bone with aluminum foil to prevent tips from burning.
3. Bake at 350° for 2 to 2 1/2 hours or until a meat thermometer inserted 2 inches into meat between ribs registers 145°. Carefully transfer roast and stuffing to a serving platter. Let pork roast stand 15 minutes before carving. Reserve 2/3 cup pan drippings for gravy.

4. Melt butter in a small saucepan over medium heat; add shallot and cook 3 to 4 minutes or until tender. Whisk in flour; cook, stirring constantly, 1 minute. Gradually whisk in wine, broth, and reserved drippings. Bring to a boil, whisking constantly. Whisk in whipping cream and 1/4 tsp. black pepper. Reduce heat to medium-low; simmer, stirring occasionally, 1 to 2 minutes or until thickened.
5. To serve, carve roast between bones using a sharp knife. Serve with gravy.

Fig-Fennel Stuffing

Makes: 13 cups
Hands-On Time: 20 min. Total Time: 1 hour, 35 min.

- 1 (16-oz.) day-old crusty Italian bread loaf, cut into 3/4-inch cubes
- 3 Tbsp. butter
- 1 red onion, chopped
- 1 cup chopped celery
- 1 small fennel bulb, chopped
- 1/3 cup Marsala
- 1 (7-oz.) package dried Mission figs, chopped
- 3 cups chicken broth
- 1 Tbsp. chopped fresh thyme
- 1 tsp. kosher salt
- 1/2 tsp. freshly ground black pepper
- 2 large eggs

1. Preheat oven to 350°. Spread bread cubes in a single layer on 2 large baking sheets. Bake at 350° for 15 minutes or until toasted. Let cool 15 minutes; transfer to a very large bowl. Increase oven temperature to 375°.
2. Melt butter in a large skillet over medium heat; add onion, celery, and fennel. Sauté 6 to 8 minutes or until tender. Add Marsala, and cook 1 to 2 minutes or until liquid evaporates.
3. Add onion mixture and figs to bread in bowl, stirring well. Whisk broth and remaining ingredients in a small bowl; pour over bread mixture, tossing well. Reserve 3 1/2 cups stuffing for pork roast. Spoon remaining stuffing into a lightly greased 11- x 7-inch baking dish.
4. Bake, covered, at 375° for 30 minutes. Uncover and bake 15 more minutes or until top is browned and crusty.

Pistachio-Crusted Rack of Lamb

Makes: 8 servings
Hands-On Time: 18 min. Total Time: 1 hour

A simple sauce of apricot preserves and whole grain mustard provides the finishing touch to the nutty crunch of the lamb coating.

- 3 garlic cloves
- 1 (³/₄-oz.) French bread baguette slice, torn
- ¹/₂ cup pistachios
- ¹/₄ cup firmly packed fresh flat-leaf parsley
- 1 Tbsp. lemon zest
- ¹/₂ tsp. ground coriander
- 2 (8-rib) lamb rib roasts (2 lb. each), trimmed
- 1 tsp. table salt
- ¹/₂ tsp. freshly ground black pepper
- 2 Tbsp. olive oil
- 3 Tbsp. whole grain mustard, divided
- ³/₄ cup apricot preserves

1. Preheat oven to 450°. With food processor running, drop garlic through food chute, processing until minced. Add bread and next 4 ingredients; process until minced.

2. Sprinkle lamb with salt and black pepper. Brown 1 lamb roast 2 minutes on each side in 1 Tbsp. hot oil in a large skillet over medium-high heat. Remove lamb from skillet; repeat procedure with remaining lamb roast and oil.

3. Brush meaty side of each lamb roast with 1 Tbsp. mustard; press breadcrumb mixture into mustard. Place lamb roasts, meaty sides up, on a lightly greased roasting rack.

4. Bake at 450° for 30 to 33 minutes or until a meat thermometer inserted into thickest portion of lamb registers 130°. Remove from oven; loosely cover with aluminum foil. Let stand 10 minutes.

5. Meanwhile, stir together apricot preserves and remaining 1 Tbsp. mustard in a small saucepan over low heat, and cook, stirring often, 1 to 2 minutes or until preserves melt. Cut each roast into 8 chops, and serve with preserves mixture.

Tuscan Beef Tenderloin

Makes: 10 to 12 servings
Hands-On Time: 25 min. Total Time: 1 hour, 15 min.

Be sure to buy a trimmed tenderloin—the butcher will be able to do this for you.

- 2 Tbsp. olive oil
- 1 (6-oz.) bag fresh spinach, chopped
- ½ tsp. dried crushed red pepper
- 1 tsp. lemon zest
- ½ tsp. table salt
- 2 garlic cloves, minced
- 2 Tbsp. butter
- 1 (8-oz.) package fresh cremini mushrooms, chopped
- ⅓ cup grated Asiago cheese
- ⅓ cup finely chopped roasted red bell pepper
- ½ tsp. table salt
- ¼ tsp. freshly ground black pepper
- 1 (4½- to 5-lb.) trimmed beef tenderloin
- 2 tsp. salt
- 2 tsp. fennel seeds, crushed
- 2 tsp. freshly ground black pepper
- 6 garlic cloves, pressed

1. Preheat oven to 425°. Heat oil in a large nonstick skillet over medium-high heat. Add half of spinach to hot oil, and cook, stirring constantly, until spinach begins to wilt. Add remaining spinach, and cook 1 minute or until all spinach has wilted. Add crushed red pepper and next 3 ingredients; sauté 1 minute. Transfer to a large bowl.
2. Melt butter in skillet over medium-high heat. Add mushrooms; cook 10 minutes or until well browned, stirring once after 8 minutes. Add to spinach in bowl. Stir in cheese and next 3 ingredients.
3. Cut beef tenderloin lengthwise down center, cutting to within ½ inch of other side. (Do not cut all the way through tenderloin.) Spoon spinach mixture down center of tenderloin. Fold tenderloin over spinach mixture, and tie with kitchen string, securing at 2-inch intervals. Place on a lightly greased rack in a roasting pan.
4. Combine 2 tsp. salt and next 3 ingredients; rub over outside of beef.
5. Bake at 425° for 30 minutes or until a meat thermometer inserted into thickest portion of tenderloin registers 130° (rare). Let stand 15 minutes before slicing.

Orange-Mustard Glazed Ham

Makes: 12 servings
Hands-On Time: 10 min. Total Time: 3 hours, 55 min.

Four ingredients come together to create a sweet, delectable glaze for this traditional holiday ham.

- 1 (10- to 12-lb.) fully cooked, bone-in ham shank
- 1 (12-oz.) jar orange marmalade
- 1/2 cup pineapple juice
- 1/4 cup Dijon mustard
- 2 Tbsp. chopped fresh rosemary
  Garnish: fresh rosemary sprigs

1. Preheat oven to 350°. Remove skin and excess fat from ham; trim fat to 1/4-inch thickness. Place ham in a lightly greased roasting pan.

2. Stir together marmalade and next 3 ingredients. Reserve 1/2 cup marmalade mixture for serving. Spoon 1 cup marmalade mixture over ham. Insert meat thermometer into ham, making sure it does not touch fat or bone.

3. Bake at 350° on lowest oven rack 3 hours, 45 minutes or until thermometer registers 140°, basting with remaining preserves mixture every 30 minutes. (Cover ham with aluminum foil after 1 hour, if necessary, to prevent excessive browning.)

4. Transfer baked ham to a serving platter; serve with reserved 1/2 cup marmalade mixture.

Perfectly Paired

This holiday, let the main event rule the menu from the appetizers on down to the perfect beverages. Whether a red or white wine, let this simple list be your guide.

TURKEY—**crisp, aromatic Viognier or fruity Beaujolais**

PORK—**citrusy Pinot Gris or jammy, tannic Zinfandel**

DUCK—**dry Rosé or light, earthy Grenache blend**

BEEF—**big bold Cabernet Sauvignon or a rich Burgundy**

LAMB—**smoky, deep Syrah or dark, fruit-forward Merlot**

***Most versatile wine for the holidays ... Pinot Noir!**

Pan-Roasted Pork Tenderloin

Makes: 8 servings
Hands-On Time: 8 min. Total Time: 42 min.,
plus 8 hours for marinating

Canned green peppercorns resemble capers in appearance. You'll find them in the store with pickles and olives. Be sure to rinse them before adding to the sauce—the brine they are packed in is too strong for the sauce.

- 1/4 cup olive oil
- 2 Tbsp. fresh lemon juice
- 3 garlic cloves, minced
- 1 Tbsp. minced fresh thyme
- 1/2 tsp. freshly ground black pepper
- 1 1/2 tsp. table salt, divided
- 3 (1-lb.) pork tenderloins, trimmed
- 1 Tbsp. olive oil
- 2 Tbsp. butter
- 1/4 cup minced shallot
- 1 1/2 Tbsp. canned green peppercorns in brine, rinsed and drained
- 1/2 cup brandy
- 2 cups heavy whipping cream

1. Whisk together first 5 ingredients and 1 tsp. salt; pour into a large zip-top plastic freezer bag. Add pork; seal and chill at least 8 hours.

2. Remove pork from marinade, discarding marinade. Heat 1 Tbsp. olive oil in a large skillet over medium-high heat; add pork. Cook 8 to 10 minutes or until well browned, turning occasionally. Add 1/2 cup water to skillet. Cover, reduce heat, and simmer 12 to 18 minutes or until a meat thermometer inserted in thickest portion registers 155°. Remove pork from skillet; loosely cover with foil, and let stand 10 minutes or until a thermometer registers 160°. Drain pan drippings from skillet, and reserve for sauce.

3. Melt butter in skillet over medium heat; add shallot and green peppercorns. Cook 1 minute; remove from heat. Add brandy, stirring to loosen browned bits from bottom of skillet. Immediately ignite brandy with a long match; let flames die down. Add reserved pan drippings to skillet, and return to heat. Bring to a boil; boil 1 minute. Stir in whipping cream. Bring to a boil; reduce heat, and simmer 5 minutes or until slightly thickened. Stir in remaining 1/2 tsp. salt.

4. Slice pork, diagonally across the grain, into 1/2-inch-thick slices. Serve with peppercorn sauce.

Pomegranate Roasted Duck Breast

Makes: 8 servings
Hands-On Time: 17 min. Total Time: 37 min.

*Reducing the pomegranate juice turns it into a tart,
syrupy glaze that complements the flavors in the
spice rub on the duck breasts.*

- 1/2 tsp. table salt
- 1/2 tsp. ground coriander
- 1/2 tsp. freshly ground black pepper
- 1/4 tsp. ground cumin
- 1/4 tsp. ground cinnamon
- 8 boned duck breasts
- 3 cups pomegranate juice
- 2 tsp. balsamic vinegar
- 2 Tbsp. butter
- 1/2 cup fresh pomegranate seeds

1. Preheat oven to 400°. Stir together first 5 ingredients
in a small bowl.
2. Trim skin on duck breasts to the size of the breasts. Make
shallow cuts in skin 1/2 inch apart in a diamond pattern.
Sprinkle duck breasts with spice mixture.
3. Cook half of duck breasts, skin sides down, in a large
skillet over medium-high heat 5 to 6 minutes or until
skins are golden brown and crisp. Turn breasts over; cook
1 minute. Transfer duck breasts to a jelly-roll pan. Drain
fat from skillet. Repeat procedure with remaining half of
duck breasts.
4. Bake duck at 400° for 12 minutes or until a meat
thermometer inserted into thickest portion registers 165°.
5. Meanwhile, bring pomegranate juice and vinegar to
a boil in a large saucepan, and cook 37 minutes or until
reduced to 1/2 cup. Remove from heat; add butter, stirring
until butter melts. Serve with duck; sprinkle with
pomegranate seeds.

Southern Stuffings & Dressings

A holiday meal wouldn't be complete without a perfect Southern stuffing. This year, instead of using your signature dressing recipe, put a spin on the traditional with these delicious recipes that are sure to become new favorites with family and friends.

Herbed Grits Dressing with Leeks and Mushrooms

Makes: 8 servings
Hands-On Time: 35 min. Total Time: 2 hours, 25 min.

Croutons made from chilled cubed grits are the base of this dressing.

- 3½ cups chicken broth
- 1 cup milk
- 1½ cups uncooked stone-ground grits
- 1 cup (4 oz.) shredded white Cheddar cheese
- ¾ tsp. table salt, divided
- ¼ tsp. freshly ground black pepper
- 2 medium leeks, thinly sliced (2 cups)
- 2 garlic cloves, minced
- 2 Tbsp. olive oil
- 2 (4-oz.) packages fresh gourmet blend mushrooms
- 1½ Tbsp. chopped fresh thyme
- 1 Tbsp. chopped fresh parsley
- ½ cup whipping cream
- 2 large eggs, lightly beaten

1. Bring broth and milk to a boil in a large saucepan. Gradually stir in grits. Cover, reduce heat, and simmer 10 minutes or until thickened, stirring occasionally. Stir in cheese, ¼ tsp. salt, and black pepper, stirring until cheese melts. Spoon grits into a greased 13- x 9-inch baking dish. Chill until firm (about 45 minutes).
2. Preheat oven to 450°. Unmold grits onto a large cutting board, sliding a knife or a spatula under grits to loosen from dish. Cut grits into ¾-inch cubes. Place cubes in a single layer on a large greased baking sheet.
3. Bake at 450° for 20 minutes; turn grits cubes, and bake 10 to 12 more minutes or until crisp and browned. Remove from oven. Reduce oven temperature to 350°.
4. Meanwhile, sauté leeks and garlic in hot oil in a large skillet over medium heat 4 minutes or until almost tender. Add mushrooms and remaining ½ tsp. salt; sauté 6 minutes or until browned and liquid has evaporated, stirring occasionally. Toss together leek mixture, grits cubes, thyme, and parsley in a large bowl. Whisk together whipping cream and eggs; pour over dressing, tossing gently to coat. Spoon dressing loosely into a greased 11- x 7-inch baking dish.
5. Bake, uncovered, at 350° for 30 to 35 minutes or until browned.

Tart Cherry-Chestnut Sausage Dressing

Makes: 12 servings
Hands-On Time: 24 min. Total Time: 1 hour, 34 min.

This flavorful dressing boasts sweet Italian sausage, dried Montmorency cherries, and roasted chestnuts. Enjoy it as a moist, hearty side dish or as a stuffing for pork, turkey, or chicken.

- 1 (12-oz.) French bread loaf, cut into ¾-inch cubes
- 12 oz. Italian pork sausage, casings removed
- ⅓ cup unsalted butter
- 1 large sweet onion, chopped
- 2 celery ribs, chopped
- 1 fennel bulb, chopped
- 1 cup dried cherries, chopped
- 1 cup whole roasted and peeled chestnuts, chopped
- 2 cups chicken broth
- ½ cup dry white wine
- 2 tsp. crushed fennel seeds
- 1 tsp. kosher salt
- ¾ tsp. freshly ground black pepper
- 1 large egg, beaten

1. Preheat oven to 350°. Spread bread cubes in a single layer on a large baking sheet.
2. Bake at 350° for 10 minutes or until toasted. Cool completely (about 10 minutes). Transfer to a very large bowl. Increase oven temperature to 400°.
3. Brown sausage in a large skillet over medium-high heat, stirring often, 5 to 6 minutes or until meat crumbles and is no longer pink; drain. Add to bread in bowl. Melt butter in skillet over medium heat; add onion, celery, and fennel. Sauté mixture 8 minutes or until tender. Remove from heat; add to bread in bowl. Stir in cherries and chestnuts.
4. Combine broth and next 5 ingredients. Add broth mixture to bread, tossing well. Spoon into a lightly greased 13- x 9-inch baking dish.
5. Bake, covered, at 400° for 30 minutes. Uncover and bake 20 more minutes or until top is browned and crusty.

Chorizo Cornbread Dressing

Makes: 12 servings
Hands-On Time: 40 min. Total Time: 2 hours, 25 min.

If you don't have time to make your own cornbread, pick up some prepared cornbread from the bakery at your local grocery store. You'll need enough to equal 12 cups of crumbs.

- 3 cups stone-ground yellow cornmeal
- 1 cup all-purpose flour
- 2 tsp. baking soda
- 1 tsp. baking powder
- 1 tsp. table salt
- 2 tsp. chili powder
- 3 cups buttermilk
- 6 large eggs, divided
- 1/2 cup butter, melted
- 1 lb. fresh chorizo sausage, casings removed
- 1 cup chopped onion
- 2 jalapeño peppers, seeded and chopped
- 1 medium-size red bell pepper, chopped
- 4 cups chicken broth
- 1/4 cup chopped fresh cilantro
- 1/4 tsp. freshly ground black pepper
- 1 cup (4 oz.) shredded extra-sharp Cheddar cheese

1. Preheat oven to 425°. Combine first 6 ingredients in a large bowl. Whisk together buttermilk and 3 eggs; add to dry ingredients, stirring just until moistened. Whisk in melted butter. Pour into a lightly greased 13- x 9-inch pan.

2. Bake at 425° for 25 to 28 minutes or until golden brown and firm. Cool completely in pan on a wire rack (about 45 minutes). Reduce oven temperature to 375°.

3. Cook sausage, onion, jalapeños, and bell pepper in a large skillet over medium-high heat, stirring often, 6 to 8 minutes or until vegetables are tender and meat is no longer pink. Drain.

4. Crumble cornbread into a large bowl. Stir in sausage mixture, broth, cilantro, black pepper, and remaining 3 eggs. Spoon dressing into a lightly greased 13- x 9-inch baking dish. Sprinkle with cheese.

5. Bake, uncovered, at 375° for 35 to 40 minutes or until golden brown.

Ciabatta Pancetta Dressing

Makes: 12 to 14 servings
Hands-On Time: 35 min. Total Time: 1 hour, 35 min.

For this recipe, don't buy the typical thinly sliced pancetta. Get a few ½-inch-thick pieces from the deli instead, and cut them into a small dice.

- 1½ cups hazelnuts
- 12 cups day-old ciabatta bread cubes
- ¼ cup butter, melted
- ¾ tsp. freshly ground black pepper
- ½ lb. pancetta, diced
- 3 large celery ribs, chopped
- 3 large carrots, finely chopped
- 1 large sweet onion, chopped
- 6 garlic cloves, minced
- 1 Tbsp. chopped fresh rosemary
- 3 cups chicken broth
- 3 large eggs
- 3 Tbsp. butter, cut into small pieces

1. Preheat oven to 350°. Place hazelnuts in a single layer in a shallow pan. Bake at 350° for 5 to 10 minutes or until skins begin to split. Transfer warm nuts to a colander; using a towel, rub briskly to remove skins. Coarsely chop nuts.
2. Place bread cubes in a large bowl. Drizzle with melted butter, and sprinkle with pepper, tossing to coat. Spread in a single layer on an ungreased half-sheet pan. Bake at 350° for 15 minutes or until toasted, stirring once.
3. Sauté pancetta in a large skillet over medium-high heat 4 to 6 minutes or until browned. Add celery and next 4 ingredients; sauté 6 to 8 minutes or until vegetables are tender. Transfer mixture to a large bowl; stir in bread cubes and hazelnuts.
4. Whisk together broth and eggs; pour over bread mixture, tossing just until moistened. Spoon into a lightly greased 13- x 9-inch baking dish. Dot with butter.
5. Bake, uncovered, at 350° for 40 minutes or until golden brown.

Pecan-and-Wild Rice Stuffing

Makes: 8 to 10 servings
Hands-On Time: 25 min. Total Time: 25 min.

Prepare this stuffing and use it to fill the cavity of Cornish hens, if desired.

- ⅔ cup coarsely chopped pecans
- 3 (2.75-oz.) packages quick-cooking wild rice
- ¼ cup butter
- ½ cup chopped onion
- ½ cup chopped celery
- ⅔ cup chopped dried apricots
- ½ cup chicken broth
- 1 tsp. table salt
- 1 tsp. orange zest
- ½ tsp. freshly ground black pepper
- ¼ cup chopped fresh parsley

1. Preheat oven to 350°. Bake pecans in a single layer in a shallow pan 5 to 6 minutes or until lightly toasted and fragrant, stirring halfway through. Set aside.
2. Cook rice according to package directions. Cool slightly.
3. Melt butter in a large skillet over medium heat. Add onion and celery, and sauté 5 minutes or until tender. Stir in next 5 ingredients and reserved rice; cook 2 minutes or until liquid is absorbed. Remove from heat, and stir in parsley and reserved pecans.

Holiday Sideboard

It goes without saying that when you host a dinner party, you're hosting a variety of taste preferences. Make sure you cater to all of them with a holiday sideboard covering a range of vegetables, salads, and casseroles.

Balsamic Green Beans and Peppers

Makes: 8 to 10 servings
Hands-On Time: 13 min. Total Time: 37 min.

For convenience and a little time-saver, buy bottled balsamic glaze instead of preparing your own. Red bell pepper gives this dish an extra pop of color for presentation as well as adds a touch of sweetness. Try substituting bottled roasted red bell peppers for an extra depth of flavor.

- 1½ lb. fresh green beans, trimmed
- ⅔ cup balsamic vinegar
- 1 medium-size red bell pepper, cut into thin strips
- 2 Tbsp. olive oil
- 1 shallot, sliced
- ½ tsp. table salt
- ½ tsp. freshly ground black pepper
- ½ cup crumbled goat cheese

1. Cook green beans in boiling salted water to cover 7 minutes or until crisp-tender; drain. Plunge beans into ice water to stop the cooking process; drain.
2. Bring vinegar to a boil in a small saucepan. Reduce heat to medium, and cook 10 minutes or until reduced by half.
3. Sauté bell pepper in hot oil in a large skillet over medium heat 3 minutes or until crisp-tender. Add green beans, shallot, salt, and black pepper; sauté 4 minutes or until beans are thoroughly heated. Drizzle with vinegar, and sprinkle with goat cheese.

QUICK & EASY
Pear-and-Blue Cheese Salad

Makes: 8 servings
Hands-On Time: 10 min. Total Time: 18 min.

Prepare the dressing and toast the walnuts in advance of party time. Then, this beautiful salad will come together in just minutes.

- ¼ cup olive oil
- 2 Tbsp. sherry vinegar
- 2 tsp. honey
- ¼ tsp. table salt
- ¼ tsp. freshly ground black pepper
- ½ shallot, minced
- 6 cups loosely packed mixed salad greens
- ½ cup crumbled blue cheese
- ½ cup coarsely chopped, toasted walnuts
- ¼ cup thinly sliced green onions
- 2 ripe pears, thinly sliced

1. Whisk together first 6 ingredients until blended.
2. Place salad greens in a large serving bowl. Top with blue cheese, walnuts, green onions, and pears. Serve with vinaigrette.

Potato Gratin with Bacon and Comté

Makes: 8 to 10 servings
Hands-On Time: 22 min. Total Time: 1 hour, 10 min.

Comté cheese is a wonderful melting cheese, ideal for topping this gratin. You'll notice its outstanding flavor at first bite.

- 3¼ cups heavy cream
- 2 garlic cloves, minced
- ¼ tsp. freshly ground nutmeg
- 2½ lb. Yukon gold potatoes, peeled
- 1 tsp. table salt
- ¾ tsp. freshly ground black pepper
- 1½ cups shredded Comté cheese, divided
- 4 cooked hickory-smoked bacon slices, crumbled

1. Preheat oven to 400°. Cook cream, garlic, and nutmeg in a heavy nonaluminum saucepan over medium heat, stirring often, 5 to 6 minutes or just until it begins to simmer (do not boil); remove from heat.
2. Using a mandolin or sharp knife, cut potatoes into ⅛-inch-thick slices.
3. Arrange one-third potato slices in a thin layer on bottom of a buttered 13- x 9-inch baking dish. Sprinkle with ¼ tsp. salt, ¼ tsp. black pepper, ½ cup cheese, and one-third crumbled bacon. Repeat layers twice. (Do not sprinkle last ½ cup cheese over top layer.)
4. Pour hot cream mixture over potatoes. Sprinkle with remaining ¼ tsp. salt. Sprinkle top with remaining ½ cup cheese.
5. Bake, uncovered, at 400° for 42 to 45 minutes or until golden brown and potatoes are tender.

Rosemary-Citrus Vinaigrette

Makes: ³/₄ cup
Hands-On Time: 2 min. Total Time: 2 min.

- ¹/₃ cup fresh red grapefruit juice
  (about ¹/₂ grapefruit)
- ¹/₄ cup extra virgin olive oil
- 3 Tbsp. rice vinegar
- 1 Tbsp. honey
- 1 tsp. chopped fresh rosemary
- ¹/₂ tsp. table salt
- ¹/₄ tsp. freshly ground black pepper

Whisk together all ingredients.

QUICK & EASY
Winter Citrus-Avocado Salad

Makes: 8 servings
Hands-On Time: 16 min. Total Time: 16 min.

*Beautiful curly endive (also called frisée) and slightly bitter radicchio
are a perfect foil for winter's best juicy citrus and creamy avocado.
The Rosemary-Citrus Vinaigrette provides a delicious complement
to the fruit with a balance of sweet, acidic, and fragrant.*

- 6 cups curly endive leaves (3 heads)
- 2 cups radicchio
- ¹/₂ cup pistachios
- ¹/₃ cup firmly packed fresh parsley leaves
- 12 (6-inch-long) chives, cut into 1-inch pieces
- Rosemary-Citrus Vinaigrette
- 2 red grapefruits, peeled and sectioned
- 4 small clementines, peeled and sliced
- 2 medium avocados, sliced

Place first 5 ingredients in a serving bowl. Add desired amount
of Rosemary-Citrus Vinaigrette; gently toss to coat. Top
with grapefruit sections, clementine slices, and avocado.
Serve with any remaining dressing.

Cheesy Pimiento Corn Casserole

Makes: 8 to 10 servings
Hands-On Time: 10 min. Total Time: 1 hour, 10 min.

Unlike traditional corn casserole made with corn-bread mix, this recipe produces a creamy, cheesy casserole somewhat like a squash casserole.

- 2 Tbsp. butter
- 1/2 cup chopped onion
- 2 garlic cloves, minced
- 1 (8-oz.) block sharp white Cheddar cheese, shredded and divided
- 2 (15.25-oz.) cans whole kernel gold and white super sweet corn, drained
- 1 (14¾-oz.) can cream-style corn
- 1 (8-oz.) container sour cream
- 1 (4-oz.) jar diced pimiento, drained
- 1/2 cup self-rising yellow cornmeal mix
- 1/2 tsp. table salt
- 1/4 tsp. freshly ground black pepper
- 2 large eggs, lightly beaten
- 1/2 cup French fried onions

1. Preheat oven to 350°. Melt butter in small skillet over medium heat; add chopped onion and garlic, and sauté 3 minutes or until tender.
2. Stir together onion mixture, 1½ cups cheese, whole kernel corn, and next 7 ingredients in a large bowl. Pour into a lightly greased 11- x 7-inch baking dish. Sprinkle with French fried onions and remaining ½ cup cheese.
3. Bake at 350° for 50 minutes or until set. Let stand 10 minutes before serving.

Roasted Beets with Herbed Dijon Vinaigrette

(pictured on page 112)

Makes: 4 to 6 servings
Hands-On Time: 19 min. Total Time: 49 min.

For a colorful presentation, use both red and golden beets.

- ½ cup coarsely chopped pecans
- 3 lb. fresh beets with greens (8 medium)
- 5 Tbsp. olive oil, divided
- 2 Tbsp. chopped fresh flat-leaf parsley
- 2 Tbsp. Dijon mustard
- 1 Tbsp. red wine vinegar
- 2 tsp. chopped fresh rosemary
- 1 tsp. chopped fresh thyme
- ¼ tsp. table salt
- ¼ tsp. freshly ground black pepper

1. Preheat oven to 350°. Bake pecans in a single layer in a shallow pan 5 minutes or until lightly toasted and fragrant, stirring halfway through. Cool completely on a wire rack. Increase oven temperature to 450°.
2. Trim beet stems to 1 inch. Peel beets, and cut each into 6 wedges. Place beets in a single layer on a 17- x 12-inch half-sheet pan or shallow roasting pan. Drizzle beets with 1 Tbsp. oil. Toss to coat.
3. Roast at 450° for 30 minutes or until beets are tender, turning after 20 minutes.
4. Whisk together remaining ¼ cup oil, parsley, and next 6 ingredients in a large bowl. Add beets, tossing to coat. Sprinkle with pecans. Serve immediately.

Served Up Sizzling

Follow these tips to keep casseroles warm and cozy.

ASSEMBLE CASSEROLES AHEAD, but wait to bake until about an hour before serving.

PLACE A PIZZA STONE IN THE OVEN 5 minutes before the casserole is finished baking. When baking is complete, remove the stone from the oven and place on a heatproof surface. Keep the casserole warm by placing it on top of the stone.

COVER BAKED CASSEROLE with heavy-duty foil or a double layer of foil, and keep warm in a 200° oven for up to 1 hour. Uncover just before serving.

Savory Sweet Potato Casserole

Makes: 10 to 12 servings
Hands-On Time: 12 min. Total Time: 2 hours, 27 min.

Parmesan cheese and thyme put a savory spin on this classic holiday dish.

- 4 lb. sweet potatoes (8 small)
- 1 cup whipping cream
- ½ cup sour cream
- 1 (8-oz.) package mascarpone cheese
- 4 large eggs
- 1 tsp. table salt
- 1 tsp. freshly ground black pepper
- 1 Tbsp. chopped fresh thyme
- ¾ cup (3 oz.) shredded Parmesan cheese
- ¾ cup chopped pecans

1. Preheat oven to 400°. Place sweet potatoes on a large baking sheet. Bake at 400° for 55 minutes or until tender. Let cool 30 minutes. Peel potatoes.
2. Reduce oven temperature to 350°. Process sweet potatoes, whipping cream, sour cream, and mascarpone cheese in a food processor until smooth. Add eggs, salt, black pepper, thyme, and ¼ cup Parmesan cheese; pulse 3 or 4 times or until blended. Spoon mixture into a lightly greased 13- x 9-inch baking dish.
3. Bake, covered, at 350° for 30 minutes. Sprinkle with pecans and remaining ½ cup Parmesan cheese, and bake, uncovered, 15 minutes or until bubbly and set.

Creamed Collard Greens

Makes: 10 to 12 servings
Hands-On Time: 1 hour, 3 min. Total Time: 1 hour, 3 min.

- 2 bunches fresh collard greens (2½ lb.)
- 4 tsp. table salt, divided
- 6 thick-cut bacon slices
- 1 cup finely chopped sweet onion (about 1 small)
- 3 Tbsp. all-purpose flour
- 2 cups milk
- 2 cups whipping cream
- 1 tsp. freshly ground black pepper

1. Trim and discard tough stalks from center of collard leaves; stack leaves, and roll up, starting at 1 long side. Cut roll into ½-inch slices, and wash slices under cold running water. Drain and coarsely chop slices.
2. Bring 6 qt. water and 3 tsp. salt to a boil in an 8-qt. Dutch oven. Add collard greens; cook 3 to 4 minutes or just until softened. Drain and squeeze dry.
3. Cook bacon in a large nonstick skillet 8 minutes or until crisp; drain, reserving 3 Tbsp. drippings in skillet. Crumble bacon.
4. Cook onion in hot drippings, stirring constantly, 5 minutes or until tender, stirring occasionally. Add flour; cook, stirring constantly, 1 minute. Slowly whisk in milk and cream. Bring to a boil, whisking constantly. Stir in black pepper, remaining 1 tsp. salt, and greens; reduce heat, and simmer, stirring often, 20 minutes or until greens are tender and sauce thickens. Stir in bacon.

Butternut-Pecan Sauté

Makes: 4 to 6 servings
Hands-On Time: 18 min. Total Time: 35 min.

*Try sweet potato in this dish as a savory alternative
to sweet potato casserole topped with pecans.*

- 1   butternut squash (about 2 lb.)
- 3   Tbsp. butter, divided
- 1½ cups chopped onion
- 2   tsp. chopped fresh sage
- ½   tsp. table salt
- ¼   tsp. freshly ground black pepper
- 1   large garlic clove, minced
- ⅓   cup coarsely chopped pecans
- ½   cup (2 oz.) shredded Parmesan cheese

1. Microwave squash at HIGH 1 minute. Peel squash;
cut squash in half lengthwise. Remove and discard
seeds and membranes; cut squash into ¾-inch cubes
to measure 5 cups.
2. Melt 2 Tbsp. butter in a large nonstick skillet. Add
squash cubes, onion, and next 4 ingredients; cook over
medium heat, stirring often, 16 minutes or until squash
is tender.
3. Meanwhile, melt butter in a small nonstick skillet
over medium-low heat; add pecans. Cook, stirring
often, 5 to 6 minutes or until toasted and fragrant.
4. Sprinkle squash with cheese and pecans; cover and
cook 1 minute or until cheese melts.

Roasted Brussels Sprouts with Sage Pesto

Makes: 6 to 8 servings
Hands-On Time: 10 min. Total Time: 30 min.

*Nothing brings out the natural sweetness in vegetables
quite like roasting. If you've never been a fan of Brussels
sprouts (think childhood memories of the frozen variety),
this recipe will make you a convert: sweet, crispy Brussels
sprouts tossed in a pesto of pungent sage, bright citrus, rich
pistachios, and a sprinkling of kosher salt. Brussels sprouts
never tasted so good.*

- 2   lb. fresh Brussels sprouts
- 1   Tbsp. olive oil
- ½   cup pistachios
- ⅓   cup loosely packed fresh sage leaves
- 2   tsp. lemon zest
- 2   Tbsp. fresh lemon juice
- 1   tsp. kosher salt
- ½   tsp. freshly ground black pepper
- ⅓   cup olive oil
-     Garnishes: lemon slices, chopped pistachios

1. Preheat oven to 425°. Remove discolored leaves from
Brussels sprouts. Cut off stem ends, and cut Brussels
sprouts in half. Toss together Brussels sprouts and
1 Tbsp. oil; spread in an 18- x 13-inch half-sheet pan.
Bake at 425° for 20 to 25 minutes or until lightly browned
and tender, stirring once.
2. Meanwhile, process pistachios and next 5 ingredients
in a food processor until smooth, stopping to scrape
down sides as needed. With processor running, pour
⅓ cup oil through food chute in a slow, steady stream,
processing until smooth.
3. Remove Brussels sprouts from oven; toss with sage
pesto in a medium bowl. Serve immediately.

Baker's Dozen

These thirteen recipes can be perfect additions to any meal, from breakfast to dinner. Serve warm rolls with dinner or make loaves of breads as homemade gifts during the holiday season.

GREAT GIFT • MAKE AHEAD

Cranberry-Apple Oatmeal Scones

Makes: 1 dozen
Hands-On Time: 30 min. Total Time: 45 min.

Reminiscent of apple pie, these tasty triangles taste like fall.

  2 cups all-purpose flour
 ½ cup quick-cooking oats
 ½ cup firmly packed light brown sugar
  2 tsp. baking powder
  2 tsp. ground cinnamon
 ½ tsp. baking soda
 ½ tsp. table salt
 ½ cup cold butter, cut up
 ¾ cup peeled and finely chopped Granny Smith apple
 ½ cup sweetened dried cranberries
 ¾ cup plus 2 Tbsp. whipping cream, divided
      Parchment paper
  2 Tbsp. chopped walnuts
  1 Tbsp. turbinado sugar

1. Preheat oven to 425°. Combine flour and next 6 ingredients in a large bowl. Cut butter into flour mixture with a pastry blender or fork until crumbly. Toss in apple and cranberries. Add ¾ cup cream to flour mixture, stirring just until dry ingredients are moistened and dough forms.
2. Turn dough out onto a floured surface. Shape dough into an 11- x 9-inch rectangle. Cut dough into 6 squares; cut each square diagonally in half to form 12 triangles.
3. Place scones on a parchment paper-lined baking sheet. Brush tops of scones with remaining 2 Tbsp. cream, and sprinkle with walnuts and turbinado sugar.
4. Bake at 425° for 15 to 18 minutes or until golden brown. Serve warm or at room temperature.

Maple-Date Cinnamon Buns

Makes: 16 buns
Hands-On Time: 36 min. Total Time: 4 hours, 31 min.

These decadent cinnamon rolls are stuffed with dates and walnuts and brushed right out of the oven with maple syrup.

- 1 cup chopped dried dates
- 1 cup boiling water
- 1 (¼-oz.) envelope active dry yeast
- ¼ cup warm water (100° to 110°)
- 1 tsp. granulated sugar
- ½ cup butter, softened
- ½ cup granulated sugar
- 1 tsp. table salt
- 1 cup milk
- 2 large eggs, lightly beaten
- 4½ to 5¼ cups bread flour
- 1 cup chopped walnuts
- ½ cup very soft butter
- ½ cup firmly packed light brown sugar
- ½ cup maple sugar
- 2 tsp. ground cinnamon
- ¼ cup maple syrup

1. Stir together dates and boiling water in a small bowl. Let stand 30 minutes. Drain.

2. Meanwhile, combine yeast, warm water (100° to 110°), and 1 tsp. granulated sugar in a 1-cup glass measuring cup; let stand 5 minutes.

3. Beat ½ cup softened butter at medium speed with a heavy-duty electric stand mixer until creamy. Gradually add ½ cup granulated sugar and salt, beating until light and fluffy. Add milk and eggs, beating until blended. Beat in yeast mixture. Gradually add 4½ cups flour to butter mixture, beating at low speed until well blended.

4. Turn dough out onto a well-floured surface, and knead until smooth and elastic (about 10 minutes). Place in a lightly greased bowl, turning to grease top.

5. Cover dough with plastic wrap, and let rise in a warm place (85°), free from drafts, 1½ to 2 hours or until doubled in bulk.

6. Preheat oven to 350°. Bake walnuts in a single layer in a shallow pan 8 to 10 minutes or until toasted and fragrant, stirring halfway through.

7. Punch dough down; turn out onto a lightly floured surface. Roll dough into a 16- x 12-inch rectangle. Spread with ½ cup very soft butter, leaving a 1-inch border around edges. Stir together brown sugar, maple sugar, and cinnamon; sprinkle over butter. Sprinkle with dates and walnuts.

8. Roll up dough, starting at 1 long side; cut into 16 (1-inch-thick) slices. Place rolls, cut sides down, in 2 lightly greased 9-inch round pans.

9. Cover and let rise in a warm place (85°), free from drafts, 1 hour or until doubled in bulk.

10. Bake at 350° for 33 to 35 minutes or until rolls are golden brown. Cool in pans 5 minutes. Drizzle with maple syrup. Serve warm.

Seeded Cheese Grissini

Makes: 2½ dozen
Hands-On Time: 32 min. Total Time: 1 hour, 5 min.

Thin, crispy, and crunchy, these breadsticks are perfect for serving with soup or salad, and even make a delicious snack.

- 1 (¼-oz.) envelope active dry yeast
- ¾ cup warm water (100° to 110°)
- 1 tsp. sugar
- 3 Tbsp. extra virgin olive oil
- 2 tsp. table salt
- 2 cups bread flour
- 1 large egg white
- 1 cup (4 oz.) shredded Comté, Gruyère, or Manchego cheese
- 2 tsp. sesame seeds
- 2 tsp. poppy seeds

1. Combine yeast, warm water (100° to 110°), and sugar in a large bowl; let stand 5 minutes or until foamy.

2. Add olive oil and salt to bowl. Gradually stir in flour to make a soft dough.

3. Turn dough out onto a lightly floured surface, and knead until smooth and elastic (about 8 minutes). Place in a well-greased bowl, turning to grease top.

4. Cover dough with plastic wrap, and let rise in a warm place (85°), free from drafts, 1 hour or until doubled in bulk.

5. Punch dough down. Turn dough out onto a lightly floured surface; roll into a 15- x 10-inch rectangle.

6. Whisk together egg white and 1 tsp. water; brush over dough. Sprinkle dough with cheese, sesame seeds, and poppy seeds. Gently press toppings into dough to adhere.

7. Cut dough crosswise into 30 (½-inch) strips, using a pizza wheel. Gently twist strips, and place on lightly greased baking sheets.

8. Preheat oven to 425°. Cover and let rise in a warm place (85°), free from drafts, 15 minutes or until puffy (dough will not be doubled in bulk).

9. Bake at 425° for 11 to 13 minutes or until golden brown.

Bourbon-Spiked Maple-Bacon Mini Cakes

Makes: 12 servings
Hands-On Time: 43 min. Total Time: 2 hours, 15 min.

These mini Bundt cakes with three of our favorite ingredients—bourbon, maple syrup, and bacon—make not only a sweet treat for the family, but they're also perfect for holiday gifts. For a serious flavor boost, splurge on Benton's artisanal bacon and Grade B maple syrup; both can be ordered online from specialty stores.

- 11 **bacon slices**
- 1⅓ **cups butter, softened**
- 1¾ **cups sugar**
- 4 **large eggs**
- ⅔ **cup sour cream**
- ¼ **cup maple syrup**
- 2⅔ **cups all-purpose flour**
- 2 **Tbsp. bourbon or whiskey**
- 1½ **tsp. vanilla extract**
  Maple-Bourbon Glaze

1. Preheat oven to 325°. Cook bacon in a large skillet over medium-high heat 8 to 10 minutes or until crisp; remove bacon, and drain on paper towels.

2. Beat butter at medium speed with an electric mixer 2 to 3 minutes or until creamy. Gradually add sugar, beating 5 to 7 minutes. Add eggs, 1 at a time, beating just until yellow disappears. Stir together sour cream and maple syrup.

3. Add flour to butter mixture alternately with sour cream mixture, beginning and ending with flour. Beat at low speed just until blended after each addition, stopping to scrape bowl as needed. Stir in bourbon and vanilla.

4. Crumble 7 bacon slices; gently fold into batter. Pour batter into 12 greased and floured miniature Bundt pans.

5. Bake at 325° for 28 to 33 minutes or until a wooden pick inserted in center comes out clean. Cool in pans on wire racks 10 minutes; remove from pans to wire racks, and cool completely (about 1 hour).

6. Drizzle Maple-Bourbon Glaze over cakes. Crumble remaining 4 bacon slices, and sprinkle over glaze.

Maple-Bourbon Glaze

Makes: 1¾ cups
Hands-On Time: 8 min. Total Time: 8 min.

The glaze sets quickly so drizzle over the cakes immediately after adding the powdered sugar.

- ⅔ **cup firmly packed light brown sugar**
- ½ **cup butter**
- ¼ **cup bourbon or whiskey**
- ½ **tsp. maple extract**
- 2 **cups powdered sugar**

Combine brown sugar and butter in a small heavy saucepan; cook over medium heat, stirring constantly, 3 minutes or until bubbly. Remove from heat; whisk in bourbon and maple extract. Gradually whisk in powdered sugar until smooth, adding 1 to 2 Tbsp. water if necessary for right consistency.

Coconut Banana Bread with Rum Glaze

Makes: 1 loaf
Hands-On Time: 12 min. Total Time: 3 hours

Coconut milk, flaked coconut, and a simple rum glaze give this banana bread a tropical makeover.

- 1 cup sweetened flaked coconut, divided
- 2½ cups all-purpose flour
- 1 cup granulated sugar
- 1 tsp. baking powder
- 1 tsp. baking soda
- ¾ tsp. table salt
- 1 cup coconut milk
- 1 cup mashed ripe bananas
- ⅓ cup butter, melted
- 1 tsp. vanilla
- 2 large eggs
- 5 Tbsp. dark rum, divided
- 1 cup powdered sugar

1. Preheat oven to 350°. Place ¼ cup coconut in a single layer in a shallow pan.

2. Bake at 350° for 5 to 6 minutes or until toasted, stirring occasionally.

3. Combine remaining ¾ cup coconut, flour, and next 4 ingredients in a large bowl; make a well in center of mixture. Stir together coconut milk and next 4 ingredients; add to dry mixture, stirring just until moistened. Spoon batter into a greased 9- x 5-inch loaf pan.

4. Bake at 350° for 1 hour and 10 minutes to 1 hour and 15 minutes or until a long wooden pick inserted in center comes out clean. Pierce loaf multiple times using a metal or wooden skewer. Slowly pour 3 Tbsp. rum over loaf. Cool in pan on a wire rack 10 minutes. Remove from pan to wire rack, and cool completely (about 1½ hours).

5. Combine powdered sugar and remaining 2 Tbsp. rum in a small bowl; drizzle over loaf. Sprinkle with toasted coconut.

NOTE: For best results, stir or whisk coconut milk until well blended before measuring.

Pumpkin-Pecan Pull-Apart Loaf

Makes: 8 to 10 servings
Hands-On Time: 29 min. Total Time: 3 hours, 24 min.

For a tall, pretty loaf, be sure to evenly layer the balls of dough in the loaf pan.

- 1 (¼-oz.) envelope active dry yeast
- ½ cup warm milk (100° to 110°)
- 2½ cups bread flour
- 10 Tbsp. butter, melted and divided
- ¾ cup canned pumpkin
- ¼ cup granulated sugar
- ¾ tsp. table salt
- 1 cup firmly packed brown sugar
- ¾ cup finely chopped pecans
- 2 tsp. ground cinnamon

1. Combine yeast and warm milk (100° to 110°) in bowl of a heavy-duty electric stand mixer; let stand 5 minutes.

2. Add 2 cups flour, 2 Tbsp. melted butter, and next 3 ingredients to bowl, and beat at low speed, using dough hook attachment, 5 minutes, stopping to scrape bowl as needed. Gradually add additional flour, as needed, until dough begins to leave the sides of the bowl and pull together and become soft and smooth. Increase speed to medium, and beat 5 minutes.

3. Cover bowl of dough with lightly greased plastic wrap, and let rise in a warm place (85°), free from drafts, 45 minutes to 1 hour or until doubled in bulk.

4. Punch dough down. Turn out onto a lightly floured surface. Divide dough into fourths. Shape each dough portion into 8 equal portions.

5. Place remaining ½ cup melted butter in a small bowl. Combine brown sugar, pecans, and cinnamon in a shallow bowl. Dip dough balls into melted butter, then roll in brown sugar mixture. Place in a lightly greased 9- x 5-inch loaf pan, creating 2 layers of 16 dough balls each. Drizzle with any remaining butter in bowl; sprinkle with any remaining brown sugar mixture.

6. Cover and let rise in a warm place (85°), free from drafts, 30 to 45 minutes or until doubled in bulk.

7. Preheat oven to 350°. Bake at 350° for 40 minutes or until browned. Cool in pan on wire rack 10 minutes; remove from pan to serving plate, and cool 20 minutes. Serve warm.

Apple Fritter Pull-Apart Bread

Makes: 12 servings
Hands-On Time: 20 min. Total Time: 1 hour, 40 min.

The sweet inspiration for this recipe is a combination of an apple fritter and monkey bread.

- ½ cup butter
- ¼ cup firmly packed light brown sugar
- 1¼ cups granulated sugar, divided
- ½ tsp. vanilla extract
- 2 (16.3-oz.) cans refrigerated buttermilk biscuits
- 1 Tbsp. ground cinnamon
- 2½ cups peeled and chopped Fuji apples (2 large)
       Vanilla Glaze

1. Preheat oven to 350°. Melt butter in a medium saucepan over medium heat. Stir in brown sugar and ¼ cup granulated sugar; cook, stirring constantly, 3 minutes or until sugar dissolves. Remove from heat; stir in vanilla.

2. Cut biscuits into quarters. Stir together cinnamon and remaining 1 cup granulated sugar in a medium bowl; add half of biscuit pieces, tossing to coat. Arrange coated biscuit pieces in a lightly greased 12-cup Bundt pan; top with chopped apples. Toss remaining half of biscuit pieces in cinnamon-sugar; arrange over apples. Pour butter mixture evenly over biscuits.

3. Place Bundt pan on middle oven rack and a foil-lined baking sheet on lower oven rack. Bake at 350° for 45 minutes or until top is golden brown.

4. Carefully invert bread onto a platter, scraping any syrup in pan over bread. Let cool 10 minutes; drizzle with half of Vanilla Glaze. Let stand 15 more minutes, and drizzle with remaining Vanilla Glaze. Serve warm.

Vanilla Glaze

Makes: ½ cup
Hands-On Time: 3 min. Total Time: 3 min.

- 1 cup powdered sugar
- 1 Tbsp. milk
- 1 tsp. vanilla extract

Stir together all ingredients in a small bowl.

Chocolate-Cherry Studded Brioche

Makes: 2 dozen
Hands-On Time: 38 min.
Total Time: 5 hours, 40 min., plus 1 day for chilling

Individual chocolate-dried cherry brioche makes a perfect breakfast during the holidays. Bake in disposable paper brioche molds for charming gifts.

1	(¼-oz.) envelope active dry yeast
½	cup warm milk (100° to 110°)
3½	cups all-purpose flour
¼	cup sugar
1	tsp. table salt
5	large eggs
1	cup butter, cut up and softened
1½	cups semisweet chocolate chunks
1	cup dried tart cherries
1	Tbsp. vegetable oil
24	(3½-inch) brioche pans
1	large egg

1. Combine yeast and warm milk in bowl of a heavy-duty electric stand mixer; let stand 5 minutes.

2. Add 1 cup flour, sugar, and salt, and beat at medium speed, using paddle attachment, 2 minutes, stopping to scrape bowl as needed. Add 5 eggs, 1 at a time, beating until blended after each addition. Add 2 cups flour, beating well. Add butter, a few pieces at a time, beating just until butter is the size of small peas. Gradually add remaining ½ cup flour, beating until blended and creamy. Add chocolate and cherries; beat just until combined. (Dough will be very soft and batterlike.) Scrape dough into a well-greased bowl; brush top of dough with oil.

3. Cover dough with plastic wrap, and let rise at room temperature, free from drafts, 3 hours or until doubled in bulk.

4. Punch dough down by gently folding edges into center with a rubber spatula; cover and chill 12 hours.

5. Divide dough into 6 equal portions; divide each portion into 4 pieces. Working with 1 piece of dough at a time (keep remaining dough, covered, in refrigerator), pinch off ¼ of dough piece; roll both pieces of dough into a smooth ball. Place larger ball of dough in a buttered brioche pan; press thumb into center of dough ball in pan, forming an indentation. Press smaller ball of dough into indentation. Repeat procedure with remaining dough and brioche pans.

6. Whisk together 1 egg and 1 tsp. water; brush over dough (reserve any remaining egg mixture). Place brioche pans at least 1 inch apart on baking sheets. Cover and let rise at room temperature, free from drafts, 45 minutes or until doubled in bulk.

7. Preheat oven to 400°. Brush brioche again with egg mixture. Bake at 400° for 15 to 17 minutes or until golden brown. Remove from pans immediately to wire racks, and cool completely (about 30 minutes).

Coffee Cake Muffins with Brown Butter Icing

Makes: 1 dozen
Hands-On Time: 18 min. Total Time: 1 hour, 12 min.

The best part of a coffee cake is usually the streusel topping and icing. Get more of what you like best in these individual cakes that have streusel inside and on top.

- 2½ **cups all-purpose flour, divided**
- ½ **cup firmly packed brown sugar**
- 1 **tsp. ground cinnamon, divided**
- ⅓ **cup butter, softened**
- 1 **cup chopped walnuts**
- ½ **cup granulated sugar**
- 2½ **tsp. baking powder**
- ¼ **tsp. table salt**
- ¾ **cup sour cream**
- ⅓ **cup butter, melted**
- ¼ **cup milk**
- 1 **tsp. vanilla extract**
- 1 **large egg**
- 12 **paper baking cups**
  Vegetable cooking spray
  Brown Butter Icing

1. Preheat oven to 400°. Combine ½ cup flour, brown sugar, and ½ tsp. cinnamon in a medium bowl; add softened butter and pinch with fingers until mixture is crumbly. Stir in walnuts. Cover and chill until ready to use.

2. Combine remaining 2 cups flour, granulated sugar, baking powder, salt, and remaining ½ tsp. cinnamon in a large bowl. Make a well in center of mixture. Whisk together sour cream, melted butter, milk, vanilla, and egg; add to dry mixture, stirring just until moistened.

3. Place paper baking cups in a 12-cup muffin pan, and coat with cooking spray. Spoon half of batter evenly into cups, filling about one-third full. Spoon 1 Tbsp. streusel mixture into each cup. Spoon remaining batter evenly over streusel; sprinkle evenly with remaining streusel mixture, pressing gently, if necessary.

4. Bake at 400° for 18 to 20 minutes or until a wooden pick inserted in center comes out clean. Cool in pan on a wire rack 5 minutes. Remove from pan to wire rack, and cool completely (about 20 minutes).

5. Drizzle with Brown Butter Icing.

Brown Butter Icing

Makes: ⅔ cup
Hands-On Time: 5 min. Total Time: 12 min.

The easy thing about this icing is that the butter is browned in the microwave. Microwaves vary in wattage, so cook the butter the lesser time, and then watch closely for browning.

- ¼ **cup butter, cut into pieces**
- 1½ **cups powdered sugar**
- 1 **tsp. vanilla extract**
- 1 to 2 **Tbsp. milk**

Place butter in a 1-qt. microwave-safe bowl or 4-cup glass measuring cup; cover with a paper plate. Microwave at HIGH 3 minutes to 3 minutes and 30 seconds or just until solids in bottom of bowl turn light brown, swirling butter in bowl after 3 minutes. Let cool 5 minutes. Add powdered sugar, vanilla, and 1 Tbsp. milk. Whisk until smooth. Add additional milk, 1 tsp. at a time, if necessary, until drizzling consistency. Use immediately.

Savory Pancetta-Gruyère Rolls

Makes: 16 rolls
Hands-On Time: 1 hour, 5 min. Total Time: 7 hours

Pancetta, Gruyère cheese, and caramelized onions make these European-style rolls anything but ordinary.

- ½ lb. thinly sliced pancetta
- ¼ cup butter
- 2 medium-size sweet onions, coarsely chopped
- 1 (¼-oz.) envelope active dry yeast
- 1⅓ cups warm water (100° to 110°)
- 3 cups bread flour
- 2 tsp. sugar
- 1 tsp. table salt
- 2 cups plus 1 Tbsp. all-purpose flour, divided
- 2 cups shredded Gruyère cheese
  Parchment paper
- 1 large egg, lightly beaten

1. Cook pancetta, in batches, in a large skillet over medium-high heat 7 to 8 minutes or until crisp; remove pancetta, and drain on paper towels. Crumble pancetta. Wipe skillet clean.

2. Melt butter in skillet over medium heat; add onions, and cook, stirring often, 20 minutes or until onions are caramel-colored. Remove skillet from heat; let cool 30 minutes.

3. Combine yeast and warm water (100° to 110°) in bowl of a heavy-duty electric stand mixer; let stand 5 minutes or until foamy.

4. Add 2 cups bread flour, sugar, and salt to bowl, and beat at low speed, using dough hook attachment, about 3 minutes. Gradually add remaining 1 cup bread flour and ½ cup all-purpose flour until dough begins to leave the sides of the bowl and pull together and becomes soft and smooth. (Note: The dough will take on a shaggy appearance as the flour is being added. When enough flour has been added, the dough will look soft and smooth, not wet and sticky or overly dry with a rough surface.)

5. Toss together cheese with 1 Tbsp. all-purpose flour in a small bowl. Add cheese mixture, pancetta, and caramelized onions to dough; beat at low speed 2 minutes or until combined. Gradually add remaining 1½ cups all-purpose flour, beating well. Increase speed to medium, and beat 3 minutes or until dough is smooth. Place in a well-greased bowl, turning to grease top.

6. Cover dough with plastic wrap, and let rise in a warm place (85°), free from drafts, 1½ to 2 hours or until tripled in bulk.

7. Punch dough down. Cover with plastic wrap, and let rise in a warm place (85°), free from drafts, 1 hour or until doubled in bulk. Punch dough down. (Note: Dough can be refrigerated overnight at this point, then brought to room temperature before proceeding to step 8).

8. Turn dough out onto a lightly floured surface. Shape dough into 16 (3½-inch) balls, and place 3 inches apart on parchment paper-lined large baking sheets.

9. Cover and let rise in a warm place (85°), free from drafts, 1 hour or until doubled in bulk. Whisk together egg and 2 tsp. water. Brush tops of rolls with egg mixture.

10. Preheat oven to 400°. Bake at 400° for 25 minutes or until golden brown and crusty. Cool on a wire rack 30 minutes.

Stollen

Makes: 2 loaves
Hands-On Time: 28 min. Total Time: 4 hours, 52 min.

Stollen is a traditional German Christmas bread. It's sweet, rich, and full of dried fruit, nuts, and candied citrus peel.

- ½ cup dried cherries
- ½ cup golden raisins
- ½ cup chopped dried apricots
- ½ cup brandy
- 1 (¼-oz.) envelope active dry yeast
- ¾ cup warm milk (100° to 110°)
- 3½ to 4 cups all-purpose flour
- ¼ cup granulated sugar
- ¼ tsp. table salt
- ¼ tsp. freshly grated nutmeg
- 6 Tbsp. butter, melted
- 2 tsp. orange zest
- 2 large eggs, lightly beaten
- ¾ cup slivered almonds
- ¼ cup chopped candied orange peel
- ¼ cup chopped candied lemon peel
  Parchment paper
- 1 large egg, lightly beaten
- ¼ cup butter, melted
  Powdered sugar

1. Combine first 4 ingredients in a small saucepan. Bring to a simmer over medium heat; remove from heat. Cover and let stand 1 hour. Drain.

2. Stir together yeast and warm milk in a 1-cup glass measuring cup; let stand 5 minutes.

3. Combine 3½ cups flour and next 3 ingredients in a large bowl. Stir in yeast mixture, 6 Tbsp. melted butter, orange zest, and 2 eggs until mixture forms a dough. Turn dough out onto a well-floured surface, and knead until smooth and elastic (about 4 to 5 minutes), gradually adding ¼ cup flour as needed.

4. Add soaked fruit, almonds, and candied orange and lemon peel to dough. Continue kneading dough until well blended, adding remaining ¼ cup flour. Place dough in a lightly greased large bowl, turning to grease top. Cover and let rise in a warm place (85°), free from drafts, 1 to 1½ hours or until doubled in bulk.

5. Punch dough down; turn out onto a lightly floured surface. Divide dough in half. Roll each portion into an 11- x 8-inch oval. Fold one short end toward center; fold other short end toward center until it overlaps first end. Place loaves, seam sides down, on a parchment paper-lined baking sheet. Cover and let rise in a warm place (85°), free from drafts, 1 hour or until doubled in bulk.

6. Preheat oven to 350°. Brush loaves with beaten egg. Bake at 350° for 35 to 40 minutes or until golden. Cool on baking sheet on a wire rack 10 minutes. Remove from baking sheet to wire rack. Brush with ¼ cup melted butter; sprinkle generously with powdered sugar. Serve warm or cool completely (about 2 hours).

Blue Cheese-Pecan Popovers

Makes: 1 dozen
Hands-On Time: 16 min. Total Time: 1 hour, 46 min.

Any leftover popovers are great for breakfast the next day. Place them on a baking sheet, and bake at 375° for 5 minutes. Spread with fig jam and enjoy!

- ¼ cup pecans, finely chopped
- 6 large eggs
- 2 cups all-purpose flour
- 2 cups milk
- ¼ cup butter, melted and divided
- ½ tsp. table salt
- 2 Tbsp. chopped fresh chives
- 2 oz. crumbled Roquefort cheese

1. Preheat oven to 350°. Bake pecans in a single layer in a shallow pan 8 to 10 minutes or until toasted and fragrant, stirring halfway through.
2. Increase oven temperature to 375°. Process eggs, flour, milk, 2 Tbsp. butter, and salt in a blender until smooth, stopping to scrape down sides as needed.
3. Grease popover pans with remaining 2 Tbsp. butter. Pour batter evenly into prepared pans, filling three-fourths full. Sprinkle with chives, cheese, and pecans.
4. Bake at 375° for 40 to 45 minutes or until browned and puffy. Pierce each popover in several places with a thin wooden skewer. Bake 5 more minutes or until crisp. Serve immediately.

Southern Anadama Bread

Makes: 16 servings
Hands-On Time: 26 min. Total Time: 3 hours, 46 min.

- 1 (¼-oz.) envelope active dry yeast
- ½ cup warm water (100° to 110°)
- 1 tsp. sugar
- ½ cup boiling water
- ½ cup molasses
- 3 Tbsp. butter
- 2 tsp. table salt
- ½ cup regular grits
- 3 to 3½ cups bread flour
- 1 large egg white, lightly beaten
  Whipped Honey-Rosemary Butter

1. Combine yeast, warm water (100° to 110°), and sugar in a small bowl. Let stand 5 minutes or until foamy.
2. Stir together boiling water and next 3 ingredients in a large bowl until butter melts. Gradually stir in grits; let cool to 100° to 110° (about 4 minutes). Stir in yeast mixture. Stir in 3 cups flour, 1 cup at a time, until dough is smooth, but not sticky. Turn dough out onto a lightly floured surface, and knead until smooth and elastic, adding remaining ½ cup flour, if necessary, to prevent sticking.
3. Place dough in a large oiled bowl, turning to coat top. Cover and let rise in a warm place (85°), free from drafts, 1 hour or until doubled in bulk. Punch dough down; turn out onto a lightly floured surface, and knead several times. Roll dough into a 14- x 7-inch rectangle. Starting at 1 short side, roll up dough jelly-roll fashion, ending seam side down. Fold ends under, and pinch seam to seal. Place dough, seam side down, in a greased 9- x 5-inch loaf pan. Cover and let rise in a warm place (85°), free from drafts, 50 minutes, or until doubled in bulk.
4. Preheat oven to 375°. Brush top of dough with egg white and make several shallow slashes diagonally across top of loaf with a knife. Bake at 375° for 45 minutes or until bread is dark brown and sounds hollow when tapped. Remove bread from pan; let cool completely on a wire rack. Serve with Whipped Honey-Rosemary Butter.

Whipped Honey-Rosemary Butter

Makes: ½ cup
Hands-On Time: 4 min. Total Time: 4 min.

- ½ cup butter, softened
- 2 Tbsp. honey
- 1 Tbsp. chopped fresh rosemary

Beat butter and honey at medium speed with an electric mixer until fluffy. Add rosemary; beat until blended.

Save Room for Dessert

Every meal deserves a sweet ending, so make sure yours doesn't disappoint. And with these delectable desserts, it will be hard not to delight. Guests will surely save room for dessert after seeing these wintry treats.

Salted Caramel Black Bottom Cheesecake

Makes: 12 servings
Hands-On Time: 33 min.
Total Time: 3 hours, 53 min., plus 1 day for chilling

Sweet, salty, chocolaty, gooey—what's not to love about this showstopping cheesecake?

5	cups mini-pretzel twists
3	Tbsp. granulated sugar
3/4	cup butter, melted
1	cup semisweet chocolate morsels
1/2	cup whipping cream
3/4	cup jarred caramel sauce
1	tsp. coarse sea salt
2	(8-oz.) packages cream cheese, softened
1	cup granulated sugar
2	(8-oz.) containers mascarpone cheese, softened
4	large eggs
2	Tbsp. all-purpose flour
1 1/2	tsp. vanilla extract
	Star-shaped cookie cutters
4	(2-oz.) chocolate candy coating squares
	Parchment paper
	Coarse sea salt or sea salt flakes
	White sparkling sugar

1. Preheat oven to 325°. Process pretzels and 3 Tbsp. granulated sugar in a food processor until pretzels are coarsely crushed. With processor running, pour butter through food chute; process until pretzels are finely crushed. Press mixture on bottom and 1 inch up sides of a 9-inch springform pan.

2. Microwave chocolate morsels and whipping cream in a small microwave-safe bowl at HIGH 1 minute or until melted; stir until smooth. Spread chocolate mixture over crust. Freeze 10 minutes.

3. Stir together caramel sauce and 1 tsp. salt. Beat cream cheese and 1 cup granulated sugar at medium speed with an electric mixer until creamy. Add mascarpone cheese, beating until blended. Add caramel sauce, beating until blended. Add eggs, 1 at a time, beating just until yellow disappears. Stir in flour until just blended. Stir in vanilla. Pour into prepared crust.

4. Bake at 325° for 1 hour and 25 minutes or until edges are set and center is almost set. Remove cheesecake from oven; gently run a knife around edge of cheesecake to loosen. Cool completely on a wire rack (about 2 hours). Cover and chill 8 hours. Remove sides of pan.

5. Microwave candy coating in a microwave-safe bowl at MEDIUM (50% power) 1 1/2 to 2 minutes or until melted.

6. Arrange star cookie cutters on a parchment paper-lined baking sheet. Pour melted candy coating to depth of 1/4 inch into cookie cutters, using a wooden pick to spread to corners. Sprinkle lightly with sea salt and sparkling sugar.

7. Freeze 10 minutes or until set. Carefully remove candy coating from cutters. Decorate top of cheesecake with stars.

Mini Red Velvet Cakes with Mascarpone Frosting

Makes: 6 servings
Hands-On Time: 26 min. Total Time: 1 hour, 36 min.

Classic red velvet cake takes on a new twist as decadent mini desserts.

- 3½ cups all-purpose soft-wheat flour
- 1¾ cups granulated sugar
- 2 Tbsp. unsweetened cocoa
- 1½ tsp. baking soda
- 1¼ tsp. table salt
- 1⅓ cups buttermilk
- 1 cup vegetable oil
- 1 Tbsp. apple cider vinegar
- 2 tsp. vanilla extract
- 3 large eggs
- 1 (1-oz.) bottle red liquid food coloring
  Mascarpone Frosting
  Garnishes: fresh raspberries, fresh mint leaves (pictured here), assorted peppermint candies (pictured on cover)

1. Preheat oven to 350°. Stir together first 5 ingredients in a large bowl; make a well in center of mixture. Whisk together buttermilk and next 5 ingredients; add to flour mixture, stirring just until dry ingredients are moistened. Pour batter into a lightly greased and floured 13- x 9-inch pan.

2. Bake at 350° for 30 to 35 minutes or until a wooden pick inserted in center comes out clean. Cool in pan on a wire rack 10 minutes; remove from pan to wire rack, and cool completely (about 30 minutes).

3. Cut cake into 6 rounds using a 3½-inch round cutter. Reserve remaining cake trimmings for another use. Split each mini cake in half horizontally. Spread about ⅓ cup Mascarpone Frosting between layers; spread remaining frosting on tops of cakes. Store cakes in refrigerator until ready to serve.

Mascarpone Frosting

Makes: 3¾ cups
Hands-On Time: 5 min. Total Time: 5 min.

- 1 (3-oz.) package cream cheese, softened
- ¼ cup butter, softened
- 5⅓ cups powdered sugar
- 1 (8-oz.) package mascarpone cheese
- 2 tsp. vanilla extract

Beat cream cheese and butter at medium speed with an electric mixer until creamy; gradually add powdered sugar, beating at low speed until blended after each addition. Add mascarpone and vanilla, beating until blended.

RED VELVET LAYER CAKE: Pour batter into 3 greased and floured 8-inch round cake pans. Bake at 350° for 28 to 30 minutes or until a wooden pick inserted in center comes out clean. Cool in pans on wire racks 10 minutes; remove from pans to wire racks, and cool completely (about 30 minutes). Spread Mascarpone Frosting between layers and on top of cake. Store in refrigerator until ready to serve.

Peppermint Red Velvet Bundt Cakes

Makes: 12 cakes
Hands-On Time: 35 min. Total Time: 2 hours, 15 min.

Miniature red velvet cakes with a peppermint-cream cheese swirl are drizzled with snow white glaze and sprinkled with chocolate curls for a showstopping and palate-pleasing holiday finish.

- 1 **cup butter, softened**
- 2½ **cups sugar**
- 6 **large eggs**
- 3 **cups all-purpose flour**
- ¼ **tsp. baking soda**
- 1 **(8-oz.) container sour cream**
- 2 **tsp. vanilla extract**
- 1 **(8-oz.) package cream cheese, softened**
- 1 **(4-oz.) white chocolate baking bar, melted**
- ½ **tsp. peppermint extract**
- ¼ **cup unsweetened cocoa**
- 3 **Tbsp. red liquid food coloring (1½ oz.)**
- **Powdered Sugar Glaze**
- **Garnish: red-and-white chocolate curls**

1. Preheat oven to 325°. Beat butter at medium speed with an electric mixer until creamy. Gradually add sugar, beating until light and fluffy. Add eggs, 1 at a time, beating just until blended after each addition.
2. Stir together flour and baking soda; add to butter mixture alternately with sour cream, beginning and ending with flour mixture. Beat at low speed until blended after each addition, stopping to scrape bowl as needed. Stir in vanilla.
3. Beat cream cheese, melted white chocolate, and peppermint extract at medium speed with an electric mixer until creamy. Add 1 cup cake batter to cream cheese mixture, beating just until blended.
4. Add cocoa to remaining cake batter; stir well. Stir in red food coloring. Spoon two-thirds red velvet batter evenly into 12 (¾-cup) greased and floured miniature Bundt pans. Drop cream cheese batter by tablespoonfuls onto red velvet batter in pans. Spoon remaining red velvet batter over cream cheese batter; gently swirl with a knife.
5. Bake at 325° for 25 to 28 minutes or until a wooden pick inserted in center comes out clean. Cool in pans on wire racks 10 minutes; remove from pans to wire racks, and cool completely (about 1 hour).
6. Drizzle cooled cakes with Powdered Sugar Glaze.

Powdered Sugar Glaze

Makes: 1½ cups
Hands-On Time: 2 min. Total Time: 2 min.

- 3½ **cups powdered sugar**
- ⅓ **cup milk**
- ½ **tsp. vanilla extract**

Whisk together all ingredients in a medium bowl until smooth.

Dried Cherry Rice Pudding

Makes: 6 servings
Hands-On Time: 34 min. Total Time: 34 min.

Arborio rice lends a creamy texture to this warm pudding.

- ½ cup sweetened flaked coconut
- 1½ cups uncooked Arborio rice (short-grain)
- 1½ cups coconut water
- 2 star anise
- ⅛ tsp. table salt
- 4 cups milk, heated
- 1 cup dried cherries
- 2 Tbsp. turbinado sugar
- ½ cup coarsely chopped roasted salted pistachios
  Garnishes: fresh cherries, additional turbinado sugar

1. Preheat oven to 350°. Place coconut in a single layer in a shallow pan. Bake 5 to 6 minutes or until toasted, stirring occasionally.

2. Bring rice, coconut water, star anise, and salt to a boil in a large saucepan over medium-high heat; cover, reduce heat to low, and simmer 8 to 10 minutes or until water is absorbed. Remove star anise.

3. Add 2 cups milk and cherries to rice mixture; cook over medium heat, stirring constantly, until liquid is absorbed. Repeat procedure with remaining milk, 1 cup at a time. Stir in 2 Tbsp. turbinado sugar during last 5 minutes of cooking. (Total cooking time is about 15 minutes.) Remove from heat.

4. Spoon into serving dishes; top each with toasted coconut, and sprinkle with pistachios.

NOTE: We tested with Sugar in the Raw turbinado sugar.

Eggnog Cream Pie

Makes: 8 servings
Hands-On Time: 28 min. Total Time: 1 hour, 24 min., plus 1 day for chilling

This pie is every eggnog lover's dream: creamy eggnog custard filling with a touch of bourbon. For those who like their eggnog spiked, add 2 Tbsp. bourbon to the whipped cream.

1³/₄ cups graham cracker crumbs (about 12 cracker sheets)
¼ cup firmly packed light brown sugar
6 Tbsp. butter, melted
2 cups refrigerated eggnog
½ cup milk
¼ cup granulated sugar
3 Tbsp. cornstarch
¼ tsp. freshly ground nutmeg
⅛ tsp. table salt
4 egg yolks
3 Tbsp. bourbon or whiskey
1 cup whipping cream
2 Tbsp. powdered sugar
2 tsp. vanilla extract
Garnish: freshly ground nutmeg

1. Preheat oven to 350°. Stir together graham cracker crumbs, brown sugar, and melted butter; press firmly into a lightly greased 9-inch deep-dish pie plate.
2. Bake at 350° for 10 to 12 minutes or until lightly browned. Cool completely on a wire rack (about 45 minutes).
3. Whisk together eggnog and next 6 ingredients in a heavy saucepan. Bring to a boil over medium heat, whisking constantly. Boil, whisking constantly, 1 to 1½ minutes or until thickened. Remove pan from heat. Whisk in bourbon.
4. Place pan in ice water; whisk custard occasionally until cool. Pour custard into crust.
5. Beat whipping cream until foamy; gradually add powdered sugar and vanilla, beating until stiff peaks form. Spread over pie. Cover loosely, and chill overnight.

Peanut Butter Brownie Cheesecake Pie

Makes: 8 servings
Hands-On Time: 26 min. Total Time: 5 hours, 11 min.

Rich, dense, and delicious, this pie is a chocolate-peanut butter fan favorite. Be sure to prepare the brownie mix according to the directions for fudgy brownies, not cakelike.

- 1/2 (14.1-oz.) package refrigerated piecrusts
- 1 (8-oz.) package cream cheese, softened
- 1/2 cup creamy peanut butter
- 1/4 cup sugar
- 1 large egg
- 1 tsp. vanilla extract
- 1 (18-oz.) package triple chocolate brownie mix
  Water, vegetable oil, and eggs as called for on brownie mix package directions for fudgy brownies
- 1/3 cup chopped cocktail nuts
- 1/2 cup miniature peanut butter cup candies, cut in half (optional)

1. Preheat oven to 350°. Fit piecrust into a 9-inch deep-dish pie plate according to package directions; fold edges under, and crimp. Chill until ready to use.
2. Beat cream cheese, peanut butter, and sugar in a medium bowl at medium speed with an electric mixer until smooth. Add egg, beating just until blended. Stir in vanilla.
3. Prepare brownie mix batter according to package directions for fudgy brownies, using water, vegetable oil, and eggs. Spread half of brownie batter in bottom of piecrust; dollop peanut butter mixture over batter, and gently spread to edge of piecrust. Dollop remaining half of brownie batter over peanut butter mixture; gently spread to edge of crust. Sprinkle cocktail nuts around edge of pie.
4. Bake at 350° for 43 to 45 minutes or until a wooden pick inserted in center comes out with a few moist crumbs. Cool on a wire rack 1 hour. Cover and chill at least 3 hours. Sprinkle miniature peanut butter cup candies in center of pie before serving, if desired.

Mocha-Hazelnut Dacquoise

Makes: 10 to 12 servings
Hands-On Time: 33 min.
Total Time: 3 hours, 48 min., plus 1 day for chilling

Look for hazelnuts without the skin. If you can only find them with skins, rub in a clean kitchen towel after toasting to remove the skins. Gently fold the ground hazelnuts into the egg whites to prevent them from deflating.

  Parchment paper
- 1 1/4 cups hazelnuts
- 3/4 cup powdered sugar
- 1 Tbsp. cornstarch
- 6 egg whites
- 1/2 tsp. cream of tartar
- 3/4 cup granulated sugar
  Mocha Cream Filling
  Chocolate shavings

1. Line 2 large baking sheets with parchment paper. Draw 2 (8-inch) circles on each sheet of parchment by tracing an 8-inch round cake pan. Turn parchment paper over.
2. Preheat oven to 350°. Bake hazelnuts in a single layer in a shallow pan 8 to 10 minutes or until lightly toasted and fragrant, stirring halfway through. Cool completely (about 20 minutes). Reduce oven temperature to 275°.
3. Coarsely chop 1/4 cup hazelnuts for top of cake. Process remaining 1 cup hazelnuts, powdered sugar, and cornstarch in a food processor until hazelnuts are finely ground.
4. Beat egg whites and cream of tartar at high speed with an electric mixer until foamy. Gradually add granulated sugar, 1 Tbsp. at a time, beating until stiff peaks form and sugar dissolves (about 2 to 4 minutes). Gently fold in ground hazelnut mixture in 4 additions.
5. Spoon one-fourth meringue batter into center of each circle on parchment paper-lined baking sheets. Spread evenly to edges of each circle using a small offset spatula.
6. Bake at 275° for 1 hour and 15 minutes or until crisp and lightly golden. Turn off oven; let meringues stand in closed oven 1 hour. Remove from oven; cool completely on baking sheets on wire racks (about 30 minutes). Carefully peel off parchment paper.
7. Place 1 meringue on a serving plate. Top with one-fourth Mocha Cream Filling, spreading almost to edges of meringue. Repeat layers twice. Top with remaining meringue layer. Spread remaining Mocha Cream Filling on top of meringue. Sprinkle with chopped hazelnuts and chocolate shavings. Cover and chill 8 to 24 hours before serving.

Mocha Cream Filling

Makes: 5 cups
Hands-On Time: 10 min. Total Time: 40 min.

- 2 (4-oz.) semisweet chocolate baking bars, chopped
- 3 cups heavy whipping cream, divided
- 1/4 cup powdered sugar
- 2 Tbsp. coffee liqueur
- 1 Tbsp. instant espresso

1. Place chopped chocolate in a large bowl. Bring 3/4 cup cream to a simmer in a small saucepan over medium-high heat. Pour cream over chocolate; let stand 1 minute. Whisk until chocolate is melted and smooth. Cool to room temperature (about 30 minutes).
2. Beat chocolate mixture, sugar, liqueur, espresso, and remaining 2 1/4 cups cream at high speed with an electric mixer until stiff peaks form.

White German Chocolate Cake
Makes: 12 servings
Hands-On Time: 31 min. Total Time: 2 hours, 50 min.

This variation of a German chocolate cake is wonderfully dense and moist. It will keep for up to 1 week, covered, in the refrigerator.

 Parchment paper
1 (4-oz.) white chocolate baking bar, chopped
1/4 cup milk
2 1/2 cups all-purpose flour
1 tsp. baking soda
1/4 tsp. table salt
1 cup butter, softened
1 cup granulated sugar
4 large eggs, separated
2 tsp. vanilla extract
1 cup buttermilk
 Coconut-Pecan Frosting
 Garnish: white chocolate curls

1. Preheat oven to 350°. Lightly grease 3 (9-inch) round cake pans; line bottoms with parchment paper, and lightly grease paper.
2. Microwave white chocolate and milk in a medium-size microwave-safe bowl at HIGH for 30 to 45 seconds or until chocolate is melted and smooth, stirring once halfway through. Cool 5 minutes.
3. Combine flour and next 2 ingredients in a medium bowl.
4. Beat butter at medium speed with an electric mixer until creamy; gradually add sugar, beating until light and fluffy. Add egg yolks, 1 at a time, beating just until blended after each addition. Add chocolate mixture and vanilla; beat on low speed until blended. Add flour mixture alternately with buttermilk, beginning and ending with flour mixture. Beat at low speed just until blended after each addition.
5. Beat egg whites at high speed until medium-stiff peaks form; gently fold into batter. Spoon batter into prepared pans.
6. Bake at 350° for 20 to 22 minutes or until a wooden pick inserted in center comes out clean. Cool in pans on wire racks 10 minutes; remove from pans to wire racks. Carefully remove parchment paper, and discard. Cool completely (about 1 hour).
7. Spread Coconut-Pecan Frosting between layers and on top and sides of cake.

Coconut-Pecan Frosting
Makes: 5 1/2 cups
Hands-On Time: 20 min. Total Time: 1 hour, 35 min.

2 1/2 cups chopped pecans
3 (5-oz.) cans evaporated milk
1 1/4 cups granulated sugar
1 cup butter
2/3 cup firmly packed light brown sugar
5 large egg yolks, lightly beaten
3 1/2 cups sweetened flaked coconut
1 Tbsp. vanilla extract

1. Preheat oven to 350°. Bake pecans at 350° in a single layer in a shallow pan 8 to 10 minutes or until toasted and fragrant, stirring halfway through. Cool completely (about 20 minutes).
2. Meanwhile, cook evaporated milk and next 4 ingredients in a heavy 3-qt. saucepan over medium heat, stirring constantly, 3 to 4 minutes or until butter melts and sugar dissolves. Cook, stirring constantly, 10 to 12 minutes or until mixture is bubbly and reaches a pudding-like thickness.
3. Remove pan from heat; stir in coconut, vanilla, and pecans. Transfer mixture to a bowl. Let stand, stirring occasionally, 1 hour or until cooled and spreading consistency.

A Cake's Christmas Wish List

Sprinkle any of these festive toppings over your holiday cake to take it from showstopping to unforgettable.

FRESH BERRIES

MINT SPRIGS

CHOCOLATE CURLS OR SHAVINGS

COLORFUL CANDIES

BROKEN OR CRUSHED PEPPERMINTS

ICED COOKIES

CHOPPED OR CRUSHED COOKIES

TOASTED COCONUT

CHOPPED TOASTED NUTS

Hot Chocolate Bundt Cake

Makes: 10 to 12 servings
Hands-On Time: 14 min. Total Time: 3 hours, 3 min.

This recipe transforms one of the holiday's favorite drinks into a luscious chocolate cake.

- 2 tsp. unsweetened cocoa
- ¾ cup unsalted butter
- ¾ cup canola oil
- 1 (4-oz.) bittersweet chocolate baking bar, finely chopped
- 1½ cups sugar
- 3 large eggs, at room temperature
- 3 cups all-purpose flour
- ¾ cup sweet ground chocolate and cocoa
- 2½ tsp. baking soda
- ½ tsp. table salt
- ¾ cup buttermilk
- 1 Tbsp. vanilla extract
  Bittersweet Chocolate Ganache
- 1 cup marshmallow crème
  Bittersweet chocolate curls (optional)

1. Preheat oven to 350°. Dust a lightly greased 12-cup Bundt pan with 2 tsp. unsweetened cocoa.

2. Combine butter, oil, bittersweet chocolate, and 1 cup water in a large heavy saucepan over low heat, and cook, stirring constantly, 8 to 10 minutes or until chocolate is melted and mixture is smooth. Remove pan from heat; add sugar, stirring until blended. Let cool 10 minutes. Add eggs, 1 at a time, whisking just until blended after each addition.

3. Whisk together flour and next 3 ingredients; add to chocolate mixture alternately with buttermilk, beginning and ending with flour mixture, stirring just until blended after each addition. Stir in vanilla. Pour batter into prepared pan.

4. Bake at 350° for 45 to 50 minutes or until a long wooden pick inserted in center comes out clean. Cool in pan on a wire rack 15 minutes; invert cake onto wire rack, and cool completely (about 1 hour).

5. Transfer cake to a serving platter. Drizzle with Bittersweet Chocolate Ganache. Chill 30 minutes or until ganache is set.

6. Spoon marshmallow crème into a zip-top plastic freezer bag. Snip 1 corner of bag to make a hole about ½ inch in diameter. Pipe marshmallow crème around top of cake and down sides; sprinkle marshmallow crème with chocolate curls, if desired.

NOTE: We tested with Ghirardelli sweet ground chocolate and cocoa.

Bittersweet Chocolate Ganache

Makes: about ½ cup
Hands-On Time: 5 min. Total Time: 15 min.

- ⅓ cup heavy cream
- 2 Tbsp. unsalted butter
- 1 (4-oz.) bittersweet chocolate baking bar, finely chopped

1. Microwave all ingredients in a medium-size microwave-safe bowl at HIGH 45 to 50 seconds or until melted and smooth, stirring after 30 seconds. Let cool 10 to 12 minutes to thicken slightly.

Twice as Nice

With so many holiday leftovers, there is always the question of what to do with them. Instead of the go-to turkey-and-stuffing sandwich, try some of these recipes that will make your leftovers feel like a brand new meal.

Turkey-Spinach Lasagna

Makes: 8 servings
Hands-On Time: 40 min. Total Time: 1 hour, 55 min.

Jarred roasted red peppers, canned tomato sauce, and fresh basil
make a quick-and-easy sauce for this lasagna.

- 1 (15-oz.) container ricotta cheese
- 1 (10-oz.) package frozen chopped spinach, thawed and well drained
- 2½ cups (10 oz.) shredded mozzarella cheese, divided
- ½ cup freshly grated Parmigiano-Reggiano cheese
- ½ tsp. table salt
- ½ tsp. freshly ground black pepper
- 1 large egg, lightly beaten
- 1 (12-oz.) jar roasted red bell peppers, undrained
- 3 (8-oz.) cans tomato sauce with roasted garlic
- ¼ cup fresh basil leaves
- 12 no-boil lasagna noodles
- 3 cups shredded cooked turkey

1. Preheat oven to 350°. Stir together ricotta cheese, spinach, 1½ cups mozzarella cheese, and next 4 ingredients.

2. Process peppers, tomato sauce, and basil in a blender or food processor until smooth.

3. Spread ½ cup sauce in a lightly greased 13- x 9-inch baking dish. Top with 3 noodles, ¾ cup sauce, one-third ricotta mixture, and 1 cup turkey. Repeat layers twice, beginning with noodles. Top with remaining noodles and remaining 1¼ cups sauce.

4. Bake, covered, at 350° for 45 minutes. Uncover, sprinkle with remaining 1 cup mozzarella cheese, and bake 15 more minutes or until top is golden brown. Let stand 10 minutes.

Turkey-Andouille Sausage Chili

Makes: 8 servings
Hands-On Time: 35 min. Total Time: 35 min.

This quick and simple turkey-and-spicy sausage chili is packed full of heat and flavor. Although we used cannellini beans, kidney or pinto beans would be equally delicious. Serve with a side of hot-from-the-oven cornbread slathered with butter.

- 1 (16-oz.) package andouille sausage, halved lengthwise and cut into ¼-inch slices
- 1 Tbsp. olive oil
- 2 cups chopped onion (1 large)
- 6 garlic cloves, minced
- 1 (1.25-oz.) package chili seasoning mix
- 2 cups chicken broth
- 2 tsp. ground chipotle chile pepper
- 2 (14½-oz.) cans fire-roasted diced tomatoes
- 3 cups shredded cooked turkey
- 1 (15.5-oz.) can cannellini beans, drained and rinsed

Toppings: sour cream, shredded sharp Cheddar cheese, chopped fresh cilantro, diced avocado

1. Cook sausage in hot olive oil in a Dutch oven over medium-high heat, stirring often, 6 minutes or until browned. Add onion and garlic; sauté 4 minutes or until onion is tender.
2. Add seasoning mix, and cook 1 minute. Add broth and next 2 ingredients. Bring to a boil; cover, reduce heat, and simmer 5 minutes. Add turkey and beans; cook 10 minutes or until thoroughly heated. Serve with desired toppings.

Turkey Tetrazzini Quiche

Makes: 6 to 8 servings
Hands-On Time: 10 min. Total Time: 50 min.

Swiss chard in lieu of the usual peas adds a Southern update.

         4 oz. angel hair pasta
       1/4 cup butter
         2 cups thinly sliced Swiss chard
         1 (8-oz.) package sliced fresh mushrooms
         1 shallot, minced
       1/3 cup dry white wine
       1/2 tsp. chopped fresh thyme
      1 1/2 cups chopped cooked turkey or chicken
         1 tsp. fresh lemon juice
       1/2 tsp. freshly ground black pepper
       1/4 tsp. table salt
         1 cup all-purpose baking mix
         1 cup milk
       2/3 cup freshly grated Parmesan cheese
         2 large eggs
       1/3 cup sea salt and black pepper croutons, lightly crushed

1. Preheat oven to 400°. Prepare pasta according to package directions.
2. Melt butter in a large skillet over medium-high heat; add Swiss chard, mushrooms, and shallot; sauté 8 minutes or until chard is tender and liquid evaporates. Add wine and thyme. Cook 1 to 2 minutes or until liquid is almost evaporated. Reduce heat to medium. Add turkey, lemon juice, pepper, salt, and cooked pasta; toss gently. Transfer turkey mixture to a lightly greased 9-inch deep-dish pie plate.
3. Stir together baking mix, milk, cheese, and eggs until smooth; pour over turkey mixture in pie plate. Sprinkle with croutons.
4. Bake at 400° for 30 to 35 minutes or until set. Let stand 10 minutes before serving.

NOTE: We tested with Bisquick Original Pancake and Baking Mix.

Curried Turkey-and-Sweet Potato Pot Pie

Makes: 8 to 10 servings
Hands-On Time: 31 min. Total Time: 1 hour

Looking for a great way to recycle leftover holiday turkey? Try this twist on traditional pot pie: a sweet and savory mixture of turkey, sweet potatoes, vegetables, and pear in a curry béchamel sauce.

         6 Tbsp. butter, divided
       3/4 cup chopped celery
       1/2 cup chopped red onion
      1 1/2 tsp. kosher salt, divided
         2 medium-size sweet potatoes, peeled and cut into 1/2-inch cubes
       3/4 cup diagonally sliced carrots
         2 tsp. curry powder, divided
       1/2 cup all-purpose flour
         2 cups chicken broth
       1/2 cup half-and-half
         2 tsp. chopped fresh thyme
       1/2 tsp. freshly ground black pepper
         3 cups chopped cooked turkey
         1 firm ripe Bosc pear, chopped
       1/2 (17.3-oz.) package frozen puff pastry sheets, thawed
         1 large egg yolk

1. Preheat oven to 400°. Melt 2 Tbsp. butter in a large skillet over medium-high heat. Add celery, onion, and 1/2 tsp. salt; cook, stirring often, 5 minutes or until tender.
2. Stir in sweet potatoes, carrots, 1 tsp. curry powder, 1/2 tsp. salt, and 1/3 cup water. Cover, reduce heat to medium, and cook, stirring occasionally, 12 minutes or until potatoes are almost tender. Remove from heat.
3. Melt remaining 1/4 cup butter in a heavy saucepan over medium-low heat; whisk in flour and remaining 1 tsp. curry powder until smooth. Cook 1 minute, whisking constantly. Gradually whisk in broth; cook over medium heat, whisking constantly, 5 minutes or until thickened and bubbly. Stir in half-and-half, thyme, black pepper, and remaining 1/2 tsp. salt; pour over vegetables in skillet. Add turkey and pear, stirring gently to coat.
4. Spoon mixture into a lightly greased 3-qt. baking dish. Top with puff pastry sheet; trim pastry to fit dish. Whisk together egg yolk and 1 Tbsp. water; brush over pastry.
5. Bake at 400° for 20 minutes or until pastry is golden brown. Let stand 10 minutes before serving.

Turkey Cornbread Cobbler

Makes: 8 servings
Hands-On Time: 10 min. Total Time: 50 min.

Cheese-topped cornbread covers a Tex-Mex turkey filling, making excellent use of holiday leftovers. For authentic-tasting results, follow our lead in the Note below.

         1 medium onion, chopped
         1 poblano chile pepper, seeded and chopped
         2 Tbsp. vegetable oil
         2 garlic cloves, minced
         2 cups shredded cooked turkey
         1 (10-oz.) can diced tomatoes and green chiles, drained
         1 (7-oz.) can Mexican-style corn, drained
         1 (15-oz.) can enchilada sauce
         1 (10 3/4-oz.) can cream of chicken soup
       1/4 tsp. table salt
       1/4 tsp. freshly ground black pepper
      1 1/2 cups self-rising yellow cornmeal mix
       1/2 cup all-purpose flour
         1 tsp. sugar
      1 1/2 cups buttermilk
         2 large eggs
         1 cup (4 oz.) shredded colby-Jack cheese

1. Preheat oven to 400°. Sauté onion and poblano in hot oil in a large skillet over medium-high heat 3 to 4 minutes or until tender. Add garlic; sauté 1 minute. Reduce heat to medium. Add turkey and next 6 ingredients; cook 2 to 3 minutes or until thoroughly heated. Pour turkey mixture into a lightly greased 13- x 9-inch baking dish.
2. Combine cornmeal mix, flour, and sugar in a medium bowl. Whisk together buttermilk and eggs in a small bowl; add to cornmeal mixture, stirring until blended. Pour cornbread mixture over turkey mixture, spreading to edges.
3. Bake, uncovered, at 400° for 30 minutes or until a wooden pick inserted in center of cornbread comes out clean. Sprinkle with cheese; bake 5 more minutes or until cheese is melted. Serve warm.

NOTE: We tested with Hatch Tex-Mex medium enchilada sauce.

Share

WITH THESE 25 COOKIE RECIPES, YOU'LL
ALWAYS BE READY WITH A DELICIOUS
GIFT FROM THE KITCHEN.

25 Days of Christmas Cookie

Christmas is filled with good friends and family, cozy nights around the fire, and delicious, tasty treats.

What better way to bring in the holiday than to bake a batch of cookies—one for each day leading up to Christmas.

From cookies to biscotti to sweet bars, there's something for everyone, and they all make great presents to spread holiday cheer.

While making these cookies, you'll not only be baking treats for everyone but cultivating traditions and making memories. All recipes pair well with a warm fire and your loved ones.

Cherry-Lemon Candy Canes

Makes: 2½ dozen
Hands-On Time: 18 min. Total Time: 3 hours, 4 min.

If you prefer not to buy a bottle of cherry juice for this recipe, substitute milk and increase the red food coloring as needed.

1	cup butter, softened
2½	cups powdered sugar, divided
1	large egg
1	Tbsp. lemon zest
1	tsp. vanilla extract
2½	cups all-purpose flour
¾	cup chopped dried cherries
3	Tbsp. cherry juice
½	tsp. red liquid food coloring

1. Beat butter at medium speed with an electric mixer until creamy. Add 1 cup powdered sugar, beating until light and fluffy. Add egg, lemon zest, and vanilla; beat until blended. Gradually add flour, beating until blended. Stir in cherries. Wrap dough in plastic wrap, and chill 2 hours.

2. Preheat oven to 375°. Shape dough into 30 (5- x ½-inch) ropes. Place 2 inches apart on ungreased baking sheets; bend over tops of ropes to look like candy canes.

3. Bake at 375° for 10 to 12 minutes or until edges of cookies begin to brown. Cool on baking sheets 2 minutes. Transfer to wire racks, and cool completely (about 20 minutes).

4. Whisk together cherry juice, food coloring, and remaining 1½ cups powdered sugar in a small bowl until smooth. Drizzle over cookies.

Pretzel-Toffee-Chocolate Chunk Cookies

Makes: about 3 dozen
Hands-On Time: 28 min. Total Time: 1 hour, 38 min.

This is the ultimate salty-sweet treat.

      1   **cup butter, softened**
      1   **cup firmly packed light brown sugar**
   ½   **cup granulated sugar**
      1   **large egg**
      2   **tsp. vanilla extract**
   2½   **cups all-purpose flour**
   ¾   **tsp. baking soda**
   ¼   **tsp. table salt**
   1½   **cups coarsely crushed mini-pretzel twists**
      4   **(1.4-oz.) chocolate-covered toffee candy bars, chopped**
      2   **(4-oz.) bittersweet chocolate baking bars, chopped**
         Parchment paper

1. Preheat oven to 350°. Beat butter at medium speed with an electric mixer until creamy; gradually add sugars, beating well. Add egg and vanilla; beat well.

2. Combine flour, baking soda, and salt; gradually add to butter mixture, beating at low speed after each addition. Stir in pretzels, toffee candy, and chocolate. Drop dough by heaping tablespoonfuls 1 inch apart onto parchment paper-lined baking sheets.

3. Bake at 350° for 12 to 14 minutes or until golden brown. Cool on baking sheets 5 minutes. Transfer to wire racks, and cool completely (about 30 minutes).

Chocolate-Dipped Pecan Shortbread Squares

Makes: 4 dozen
Hands-On Time: 40 min. Total Time: 3 hours, 55 min.

For the best-tasting results, use high-quality semisweet baking chocolate.

- 1 cup pecan halves
- 1 cup butter, softened
- ¾ cup sugar
- 1 tsp. vanilla extract
- 2 cups all-purpose flour
- ¼ tsp. table salt
- 2 (4-oz.) semisweet chocolate baking bars, chopped
  Parchment paper
  Garnish: finely chopped pecans

1. Preheat oven to 350°. Bake pecan halves in a single layer in a shallow pan 8 to 10 minutes or until toasted and fragrant, stirring halfway through. Cool completely. Finely chop pecans, and set aside.

2. Beat butter at medium speed with an electric mixer until creamy; gradually add sugar, beating until well blended. Add vanilla; beat until blended. Combine flour and salt; gradually add to butter mixture, beating on low speed just until blended. Stir in pecans.

3. Divide dough into 2 equal portions; shape each portion into a 6- x 2-inch square log. Wrap tightly in plastic wrap, and chill 2 hours.

4. Preheat oven to 350°. Cut logs into ¼-inch slices. Place 1 inch apart on ungreased baking sheets. Bake at 350° for 14 to 16 minutes or until edges are golden brown. Cool on baking sheets 5 minutes; transfer to wire racks, and cool completely (about 10 minutes).

5. Microwave chocolate at HIGH 1 to 1½ minutes or until melted and smooth, stirring at 30-second intervals. Dip each cookie halfway into melted chocolate, letting excess drip off. Place on parchment paper-lined baking sheets. Let stand 30 minutes or until set.

FIX IT FASTER: Here are two ways to speed along this recipe: Freeze the dough logs 1 hour instead of chilling them, and chill the finished cookies to harden the chocolate coating.

Molasses Crisps

Makes: about 3 dozen
Hands-On Time: 24 min.
Total Time: 1 hour, 12 min.

As a decorating option, you can forego rolling the cookie balls in sugar and just drizzle the baked cookies with melted white chocolate instead.

- ½ **cup butter, softened**
- ¼ **cup shortening**
- 1 **cup granulated sugar**
- ¼ **cup molasses**
- 3 **Tbsp. minced crystallized ginger**
- 1 **large egg**
- 1¾ **cups all-purpose flour**
- 1 **tsp. baking soda**
- 1 **tsp. ground cinnamon**
- ¼ **tsp. ground cloves**
- ¾ **cup turbinado sugar**

1. Preheat oven to 350°. Beat butter, shortening, and granulated sugar at medium speed with an electric mixer until light and fluffy. Add molasses, crystallized ginger, and egg, beating just until blended.

2. Stir together flour and next 3 ingredients in a small bowl; gradually add to butter mixture, beating at low speed just until blended.

3. Shape dough into 1-inch balls; roll in turbinado sugar. Place 3 inches apart on ungreased baking sheets.

4. Bake at 350° for 12 to 14 minutes or until browned and crisp. Remove from baking sheets to wire racks, and cool completely (about 20 minutes).

Cherry-Chocolate Icebox Cookies

Makes: about 3 1/2 dozen
Hands-On Time: 18 min.
Total Time: 2 hours, 42 min.

Keep a log of this dough in the freezer for slicing and baking as needed during the holidays.

- 2 2/3 cups all-purpose flour
- 1/3 cup unsweetened cocoa
- 1/2 tsp. baking powder
- 1/4 tsp. table salt
- 1 cup butter, softened
- 1 cup sugar
- 1 large egg
- 1 Tbsp. cherry liqueur*
- 3/4 cup dried cherries, chopped
- 1 (4-oz.) semisweet chocolate baking bar, chopped

1. Stir together first 4 ingredients. Beat butter and sugar at medium speed with an electric mixer until light and fluffy. Add egg and liqueur, beating just until blended. Gradually add flour mixture, beating just until blended after each addition. Stir in cherries and chocolate.

2. Shape dough into two 10-inch logs using wax paper. Wrap tightly in plastic wrap, and chill at least 2 hours.

3. Preheat oven to 350°. Cut logs into 1/2-inch-thick slices. Place 1 inch apart on ungreased baking sheets. Bake at 350° for 12 minutes or until set. Transfer to wire racks; cool completely (about 20 minutes).

*1 1/2 tsp. vanilla extract may be substituted.

NOTE: Dough logs may be cut into 1/4-inch-thick slices, if desired. The bake time remains the same. Makes: about 6 1/2 dozen.

Gingerbread Linzer Cookies

Makes: 2 dozen sandwich cookies
Hands-On Time: 30 min. Total Time: 4 hours

Gingerbread dough is rolled and cut to resemble traditional Austrian Linzer cookies, only with festive bell-shaped centers and a lemon curd filling.

- ³/₄ **cup butter, softened**
- 1 **cup packed light brown sugar**
- ¹/₂ **cup molasses**
- 1 **large egg**
- 3 **cups all-purpose flour**
- 1 **tsp. baking soda**
- 2 **tsp. ground ginger**
- 2 **tsp. ground cinnamon**
- ¹/₂ **tsp. table salt**
- ¹/₂ **tsp. ground cloves**
- ¹/₄ **cup lemon curd or orange marmalade**
  Powdered sugar

1. Beat butter at medium speed with an electric mixer until creamy; gradually add brown sugar, beating until blended. Add molasses and egg, beating just until blended.

2. Stir together flour and next 5 ingredients; gradually add to butter mixture, beating at low speed after each addition. Divide dough into 2 equal portions; flatten each into a disk. Cover and chill 3 hours.

3. Preheat oven to 350°. Place 1 portion of dough on a lightly floured surface, and roll to a ¹/₈-inch thickness. Cut with a 2¹/₂-inch fluted round cutter. Place cookies 2 inches apart on lightly greased baking sheets. Repeat procedure with remaining dough disk. Cut centers out of half of cookies with a 1¹/₂-inch bell-shaped cutter. Place cookies 2 inches apart on lightly greased baking sheets.

4. Bake at 350° for 8 to 10 minutes or until edges are set. Cool on baking sheets 2 minutes. Transfer to wire racks, and cool completely (about 20 minutes).

5. Spread each solid cookie with ¹/₂ tsp. lemon curd. Sprinkle cookies with cutouts with powdered sugar. Top each solid cookie with a cookie with cutout.

Frosted Cranberry-Orange Cookies

Makes: about 3 1/2 dozen
Hands-On Time: 45 min. Total Time: 1 hour, 40 min.

Cranberries, oranges, and walnuts are classic holiday ingredients that flavor these cookies. Once you add icing, they become the perfect gift for friends this season.

- 1 1/2 cups firmly packed brown sugar
- 1 cup butter, softened
- 1 Tbsp. orange zest
- 1 tsp. vanilla extract
- 1 large egg
- 2 1/2 cups all-purpose flour
- 1/2 tsp. baking soda
- 1/2 tsp. table salt
- 1 cup coarsely chopped walnuts, lightly toasted
- 1 (5-oz.) package sweetened dried cranberries
- 1 1/2 cups powdered sugar
- 2 Tbsp. half-and-half
- 1/2 tsp. orange zest
  Orange zest

1. Preheat oven to 375°. Beat brown sugar and butter at medium speed with an electric mixer until light and fluffy. Add 1 Tbsp. orange zest, vanilla, and egg, beating until blended. Stir together flour, baking soda, and salt; gradually add to sugar mixture, beating until blended. Stir in walnuts and cranberries.
2. Drop dough by rounded tablespoonfuls 2 inches apart onto lightly greased baking sheets.
3. Bake at 375° for 10 to 12 minutes or until edges are lightly browned. Cool on baking sheets 1 minute. Transfer to wire racks, and cool completely (about 15 minutes).
4. Stir together powdered sugar, half-and-half, and 1/2 tsp. orange zest. Spread frosting evenly over cookies. Sprinkle with additional orange zest.

NOTE: We tested with Craisins.

Chocolate-Hazelnut Palmiers

Makes: 2 1/2 dozen
Hands-On Time: 15 min. Total Time: 1 hour, 35 min.

These simple, sweet pastries make a great gift. They're sturdy enough for mailing.

- 1/3 cup hazelnuts
- 1/2 (17.3-oz.) package frozen puff pastry sheets, thawed
- 2 Tbsp. granulated sugar
- 1/2 cup hazelnut spread
  Parchment paper
- 1 large egg, lightly beaten
- 2 Tbsp. turbinado sugar

1. Preheat oven to 350°. Place nuts in a single layer in a shallow pan. Bake at 350° for 5 to 10 minutes or until skins begin to split. Transfer warm nuts to a colander; using a towel, rub briskly to remove skins. Finely chop nuts.
2. Increase oven temperature to 425°. Unfold pastry sheet on a surface sprinkled with granulated sugar; roll into a 15- x 11-inch rectangle. Spread hazelnut spread over pastry to within 1/2 inch of the edge; sprinkle with chopped hazelnuts. Starting at each long side, roll pastry up tightly, jelly-roll fashion, to meet in center. (The shape of the roll resembles a scroll.) Wrap in plastic wrap; cover and freeze 20 minutes.
3. Cut roll into 1/3-inch-thick slices; place 1 inch apart on parchment paper-lined baking sheets. Brush tops with beaten egg; sprinkle with turbinado sugar.
4. Bake at 425° for 18 minutes or until lightly browned. Cool on baking sheets 5 minutes. Transfer to wire racks, and cool completely (about 20 minutes).

Chocolate-Pecan Pie Bar Cookies

Makes: about 2 1/2 dozen
Hands-On Time: 20 min. Total Time: 6 hours, 15 min.

Who needs a messy slice of pecan pie when you can eat these rich bars out of hand? Serve them individually wrapped in parchment paper, if desired.

- 2 cups all-purpose flour
- 1/2 cup granulated sugar
- 1/4 tsp. table salt
- 3/4 cup butter, softened
- 1/3 cup toffee bits
- 1 cup firmly packed brown sugar
- 3/4 cup light corn syrup
- 1/2 cup butter
- 1/3 cup honey
- 4 large eggs, lightly beaten
- 2 1/2 cups pecan pieces
- 1 tsp. vanilla extract
- 1 cup chopped semisweet chocolate

1. Preheat oven to 350°. Combine flour, granulated sugar, and salt in a medium bowl. Beat 3/4 cup softened butter at medium speed with an electric mixer until creamy; gradually add flour mixture, beating until blended. Stir in toffee bits. Press dough evenly on bottom of a lightly greased 13- x 9-inch baking pan.
2. Bake at 350° for 18 to 20 minutes or until lightly browned.
3. Stir together brown sugar, corn syrup, 1/2 cup butter, and honey in a 2-qt. saucepan. Bring to a boil over medium heat, stirring occasionally. Boil 1 minute; remove from heat. Stir one-fourth of hot mixture into eggs; add to remaining hot mixture. Stir in pecans and vanilla. Pour filling into prepared crust. Sprinkle with chocolate.
4. Bake at 350° for 35 to 40 minutes or until set. Cool completely in pan on a wire rack (about 1 hour). Cover and chill at least 4 hours or until firm. Let stand at room temperature 10 minutes. Cut into 16 bars. Cut bars diagonally in half.

NOTE: These bars can be cut into 24 bars.

Spiced Sorghum Snowflakes

Makes: about 7 dozen
Hands-On Time: 3 hours, 25 min. Total Time: 5 hours, 25 min.

Perfect for gift giving or tucking inside a stocking, these beautiful, crisp cookies are flavored with sweet sorghum and a blend of gingerbread spices.

- 1/2 **cup butter, softened**
- 1/4 **cup granulated sugar**
- 1/4 **cup firmly packed dark brown sugar**
- 2 **tsp. orange zest**
- 1 **large egg**
- 3 **Tbsp. hot water**
- 1 **tsp. baking soda**
- 1/2 **cup sorghum**
- 3 **cups all-purpose flour**
- 2 **tsp. ground ginger**
- 1 **tsp. ground cinnamon**
- 1/2 **tsp. ground allspice**
- 1/4 **tsp. ground nutmeg**
- 1/4 **tsp. table salt**
- **Parchment paper**
- **Royal Icing**
- **White sparkling sugar, nonpareils, sugar pearls**

1. Beat butter and sugars at medium speed with a heavy-duty electric stand mixer until fluffy. Add orange zest and egg, beating until smooth.

2. Stir together hot water and baking soda in a small bowl until baking soda is dissolved. Stir in sorghum.

3. Stir together flour and next 5 ingredients; add to butter mixture alternately with sorghum mixture, beginning and ending with flour mixture.

4. Divide dough into 2 equal portions; flatten each into a disk. Cover and chill at least 1 hour or until firm.

5. Preheat oven to 325°. Place 1 portion of dough on a lightly floured surface, and roll to 1/4-inch thickness. Cut with assorted sizes of snowflake-shaped cutters. Place cookies 1 inch apart on parchment paper-lined baking sheets. Repeat procedure with remaining dough disk. Once cookies are cut and placed on baking sheets, freezing them about 10 minutes allows them to better hold their shape during baking.

6. Bake at 325° for 13 to 15 minutes or until cookies are puffed and slightly darker around the edges. Cool on pans 1 minute; transfer to wire racks, and cool completely (about 30 minutes).

7. Spoon Royal Icing into a zip-top plastic freezer bag. Snip 1 corner of bag to make a small hole. Pipe icing in decorative designs on each cookie. Sprinkle with white sparkling sugar, and decorate with nonpareils and sugar pearls. Let icing harden at least 1 hour.

NOTE: We tested with snowflake-shaped cutters ranging in size from 1 3/4 inch to 4 inches.

Royal Icing

Makes: 3 cups
Hands-On Time: 5 min. Total Time: 5 min.

- 1 **(16-oz.) package powdered sugar**
- 3 **Tbsp. meringue powder**
- 1/2 **cup warm water**

Beat all ingredients at low speed with an electric mixer until blended. Beat at high speed 4 minutes or until glossy and stiff peaks form, adding a few drops of additional water, if necessary, for desired consistency.

Chocolate-Cappuccino Whoopie Pies

Makes: 25 whoopie pies
Hands-On Time: 28 min. Total Time: 1 hour, 28 min.

These little handheld treats are the perfect combination of not-too-sweet cookies joined together with a decadent espresso-cream cheese filling.

- 2 cups all-purpose flour
- ½ cup unsweetened cocoa
- 1 tsp. baking soda
- ½ tsp. table salt
- ½ cup butter, softened
- 1 cup firmly packed light brown sugar
- 1 large egg
- 1 tsp. vanilla extract
- 1 cup buttermilk
- Parchment paper
- Espresso Filling
- ½ cup crushed chocolate-coated coffee beans

1. Preheat oven to 350°. Whisk together first 4 ingredients in a medium bowl.
2. Beat butter and brown sugar at medium speed with a heavy-duty electric stand mixer 2 minutes or until fluffy. Add egg and vanilla; beat just until blended. Add flour mixture alternately with buttermilk, beginning and ending with flour mixture. Beat at low speed until blended after each addition, stopping to scrape bowl as needed.
3. Drop dough by tablespoonfuls 2 inches apart onto parchment paper-lined baking sheets.
4. Bake at 350° for 10 minutes or until cookies are set and tops spring back when touched. Cool on pans 5 minutes; transfer to wire racks, and cool completely (about 10 minutes).
5. Spread about 1½ Tbsp. Espresso Filling on 1 flat side of half of cooled cookies; top with remaining cookies, pressing gently. Roll edges of whoopie pies in crushed coffee beans.

Espresso Filling

Makes: 2½ cups
Hands-On Time: 5 min. Total Time: 5 min.

- 1½ (3-oz.) packages cream cheese, softened
- 6 Tbsp. butter, softened
- 1 Tbsp. instant espresso
- 3 Tbsp. milk
- 1½ tsp. vanilla extract
- 3 cups powdered sugar

Beat first 5 ingredients at medium speed with an electric mixer until smooth. Gradually add powdered sugar, beating mixture at low speed until blended.

Sugar Cookie Stars

Makes: about 3 dozen
Hands-On Time: 1 hour Total Time: 2 hours, 10 min.

Use your favorite 3-inch holiday cookie cutter if you don't have a star cutter on hand.

- 1 **cup butter, softened**
- 1 **cup granulated sugar**
- ³/₄ **tsp. almond extract**
- 1 **large egg**
- 2¹/₄ **cups all-purpose flour**
- ¹/₄ **tsp. table salt**
  White Frosting
- ³/₄ **cup light blue sparkling sugar**

1. Beat butter and granulated sugar at medium speed with an electric mixer until light and fluffy. Add almond extract and egg, beating until blended. Combine flour and salt. Gradually add to butter mixture, beating at low speed just until blended.
2. Divide dough into 2 equal portions; flatten each into a disk. Cover and chill 20 minutes.
3. Preheat oven to 350°. Place 1 portion of dough on a lightly floured surface, and roll to a ¹/₈-inch thickness. Cut with a 3-inch star-shaped cookie cutter. Place cookies 2 inches apart on ungreased baking sheets. Repeat procedure with remaining dough disk.
4. Bake at 350° for 10 to 12 minutes or until edges are lightly browned. Cool on baking sheets 5 minutes; transfer to wire racks, and cool completely (about 10 minutes).
5. Spread White Frosting over cookies. Sprinkle with sparkling sugar.

White Frosting

Makes: 3 cups
Hands-On Time: 5 min. Total Time: 5 min.

- 1 **cup butter, softened**
- 3 **cups powdered sugar, sifted**
- 3 **Tbsp. heavy cream**
- ¹/₂ **tsp. almond extract**

Beat butter and powdered sugar at low speed with an electric mixer until blended. Increase speed to medium, and beat 3 minutes. Add heavy cream and almond extract, beating to desired consistency.

NOTE: Purchase sparkling sugar at cook stores or crafts stores.

Candy Cane Biscotti

Makes: about 2½ dozen
Hands-On Time: 14 min. Total Time: 2 hours, 30 min.

*Before you drizzle cookies with chocolate, stand them
up on a wire rack set over wax paper to catch the drips.*

- ¾ cup granulated sugar
- ½ cup butter, softened
- 2 large eggs, lightly beaten
- 2½ cups all-purpose flour
- 2 tsp. baking powder
- ¼ tsp. table salt
- 1 Tbsp. peppermint schnapps
- 1 tsp. vanilla extract
- ¾ cup crushed soft peppermint sticks, divided
  Wax paper
- 1 (4-oz.) dark chocolate baking bar, chopped
  Coarse sugar

1. Preheat oven to 350°. Beat sugar and butter at medium speed
with an electric mixer until creamy. Add eggs, 1 at a time,
beating until blended after each addition. Combine flour,
baking powder, and salt; gradually add to butter mixture,
beating until blended. Stir in peppermint schnapps and
vanilla. Stir in ½ cup crushed peppermint.
2. Divide dough in half. Shape each portion of dough
into a 9- x 2-inch log on a lightly greased baking
sheet, using lightly floured hands.
3. Bake at 350° for 28 to 30 minutes or until firm.
Transfer to wire racks; cool completely (about
1 hour). Cut each log diagonally into ½-inch-
thick slices with a serrated knife, using a
gentle sawing motion. Place slices, cut sides
up, on baking sheets.
4. Bake at 350° for 10 minutes; turn cookies
over, and bake 8 more minutes. Transfer
to wire racks set over wax paper, and cool
completely (about 30 minutes).
5. Microwave chocolate in a small
microwave-safe bowl at HIGH 30 to 60
seconds or until melted and smooth,
stirring at 30-second intervals. Drizzle
chocolate over tops of biscotti; sprinkle
with coarse sugar and remaining
¼ cup crushed peppermint. Let
stand until chocolate is set.

Lemon-Glazed Spritz Cookies

Makes: 9 dozen
Hands-On Time: 40 min.
Total Time: 1 hour, 32 min.

Be sure to use ungreased baking sheets when using a cookie press so that the dough will release from the press and adhere to the baking sheets.

- 1 **cup butter, softened**
- 1 **cup granulated sugar**
- 1 **large egg**
- 2 **tsp. lemon zest**
- 1 **tsp. vanilla extract**
- 2½ **cups all-purpose flour**
- ¼ **tsp. table salt**
- **Wax paper**
- 2 **cups powdered sugar**
- ¼ **cup fresh lemon juice**

1. Preheat oven to 375°. Beat butter at medium speed with an electric mixer until creamy; gradually add granulated sugar, beating until light and fluffy. Add egg, lemon zest, and vanilla; beat well. Combine flour and salt; gradually add to butter mixture, beating on low speed just until blended.

2. Use a cookie press fitted with a wreath-shaped disk to shape dough into 1½-inch cookies, following manufacturer's instructions. Place on ungreased baking sheets.

3. Bake at 375° for 7 to 9 minutes or until edges are golden brown. Cool on baking sheets 2 minutes. Transfer to wire racks, and cool completely (about 10 minutes).

4. Place wire racks over a wax paper-lined surface. Whisk together powdered sugar and lemon juice in a small bowl until smooth. Dip tops of cookies in glaze, allowing excess to drip back into bowl. Place cookies, glazed sides up, on wire racks. Let glaze harden at least 15 minutes.

Fudgy Cookies with Peanut Butter Middles

Makes: 2 dozen
Hands-On Time: 1 hour Total Time: 2 hours, 30 min.

These are awesome chewy chocolate cookies with a peanut crunch on the outside and creamy candy inside.

1	cup sugar
3/4	cup butter, softened
1	tsp. vanilla extract
1	large egg
1	cup all-purpose flour
1/2	cup unsweetened cocoa
1	tsp. baking powder
1/4	tsp. table salt
1/2	cup chocolate mini-morsels
24	miniature peanut butter cup candies
3/4	cup finely chopped peanuts

1. Beat sugar and butter at medium speed with an electric mixer until creamy. Add vanilla and egg, beating just until blended. Stir together flour, cocoa, baking powder, and salt; gradually add to sugar mixture, beating just until blended. Stir in mini-morsels. Cover and chill 30 minutes.
2. Preheat oven to 350°. Shape dough into 1-inch balls; press 1 peanut butter cup candy in center of each cookie. Roll in chopped peanuts. (If dough becomes too soft to shape, refrigerate until firm.) Place 1 inch apart on ungreased baking sheets.
3. Bake at 350° for 13 to 15 minutes or until tops are set. Transfer to wire racks; cool completely (about 30 minutes).

GREAT GIFT • MAKE AHEAD
Cranberry-Ginger Diamonds

Makes: 4 1/2 dozen
Hands-On Time: 26 min. Total Time: 1 hour, 46 min.

Sparkling sugar adds a nice touch to the tops of these double-ginger cookies.

1/2	cup butter, softened
1/2	cup powdered sugar
1	cup all-purpose flour
1/4	tsp. table salt
1/4	cup minced crystallized ginger
1/4	cup finely chopped sweetened dried cranberries
2	tsp. grated fresh ginger
	Parchment paper
2	Tbsp. white sparkling sugar

1. Beat butter at medium speed with a heavy-duty electric stand mixer until creamy. Gradually add powdered sugar, beating well.
2. Combine flour and salt; add to butter mixture, beating until blended. Add crystallized ginger, cranberries, and fresh ginger, beating just until blended. Cover and chill 1 hour.
3. Preheat oven to 325°. Roll dough to 1/8-inch thickness on a lightly floured surface. Cut with a 2-inch diamond cutter. Place 1 inch apart on parchment paper-lined baking sheets. Sprinkle cookies with sparkling sugar; gently press sugar into dough.
4. Bake at 325° for 9 to 11 minutes or until edges are lightly browned. Cool on baking sheets 5 minutes. Transfer to wire racks, and cool completely (about 10 minutes).

Pistachio Thumbprint Cookies

Makes: 33 cookies
Hands-On Time: 25 min. Total Time: 40 min.

Flecked with green pistachios and filled with red berry jam, these thumbprints are perfectly festive.

- 3/4 **cup pistachios**
- 1 **cup butter, softened**
- 1/2 **cup sugar**
- 2 **large egg yolks**
- 1 **tsp. vanilla extract**
- 1/2 **tsp. almond extract**
- 2 **cups all-purpose flour**
- 1/3 **cup seedless strawberry or raspberry jam**

1. Preheat oven to 350°. Pulse pistachios in a food processor 10 or 12 times or until pistachios are very finely chopped.

2. Beat butter at medium speed with an electric mixer about 2 to 3 minutes or until creamy. Gradually add sugar, beating well. Add egg yolks and extracts, beating well. Gradually add flour, beating on low speed just until blended. Stir in pistachios.

3. Shape dough into 1-inch balls; place 2 inches apart on ungreased baking sheets. Press thumb or end of a wooden spoon into center of each ball, forming an indentation. Spoon about 1/2 tsp. jam into each indentation.

4. Bake at 350° for 12 to 15 minutes or until edges are golden brown. Cool on baking sheets 5 minutes. Transfer to wire racks, and cool completely (about 15 minutes).

GREAT GIFT

Lemon-Rosemary Cornmeal Madeleines

Makes: 4 dozen
Hands-On Time: 14 min. Total Time: 1 hour, 44 min.

A simple lemon glaze saturates these light sponge cakes and makes them memorable.

- 2 cups self-rising white cornmeal mix
- ½ cup all-purpose flour
- ⅓ cup granulated sugar
- 1½ cups buttermilk
- ½ cup butter, melted
- 2 large eggs, lightly beaten
- 1 Tbsp. lemon zest
- 1 Tbsp. finely chopped fresh rosemary
- 2⅔ cups powdered sugar
- ¼ cup fresh lemon juice
- ⅓ cup milk

1. Whisk together cornmeal mix, flour, and granulated sugar in a large bowl. Add buttermilk, melted butter, eggs, lemon zest, and rosemary. Whisk together just until blended. Cover; refrigerate batter 30 minutes.

2. Preheat oven to 400°. Whisk together powdered sugar, lemon juice, and milk in a medium bowl; set aside.

3. Spoon batter into lightly greased and floured shiny madeleine pans, filling three-fourths full.

4. Bake at 400°, in batches, 15 to 17 minutes or until golden brown. Remove from pans immediately; let cool slightly. Dip both sides of each madeleine in glaze; place on cooling rack, scalloped side up. Let stand until glaze sets.

EDITOR'S FAVORITE
Coconut Snowballs

Makes: about 4 dozen
Hands-On Time: 20 min. Total Time: 2 hours, 10 min.

Toasted coconut delivers an appealing texture when you bite into these buttery holiday cookies.

1	cup sweetened flaked coconut
1	cup butter, softened
2	cups all-purpose flour
1¼	cups powdered sugar, divided
1	tsp. coconut extract
1	tsp. vanilla extract

1. Preheat oven to 350°. Place coconut in a single layer in a shallow pan.

2. Bake at 350° for 5 to 6 minutes or until toasted, stirring occasionally. Cool completely.

3. Beat butter at medium speed with an electric mixer 2 minutes or until light and fluffy. Gradually add flour and ½ cup powdered sugar, beating until blended. Add extracts, beating until blended. Stir in coconut. Cover and chill dough 1 hour.

4. Preheat oven to 350°. Shape dough into ¾-inch balls; place 1 inch apart on ungreased baking sheets. Bake at 350° for 16 to 18 minutes or until bottoms are golden brown. Cool on baking sheets 5 minutes.

5. Place remaining ¾ cup powdered sugar in a bowl. Roll warm cookies in powdered sugar, tossing to coat. Transfer to wire racks, and cool completely (about 30 minutes).

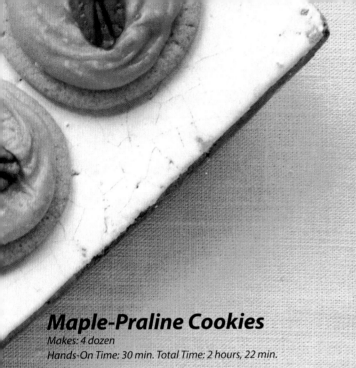

Maple-Praline Cookies

Makes: 4 dozen
Hands-On Time: 30 min. Total Time: 2 hours, 22 min.

This cookie is special enough for a cookie swap or gift giving; it's like biting into praline candy on top of a drop cookie.

- 3/4 cup butter, softened
- 1/4 cup shortening
- 1 cup firmly packed brown sugar
- 1 Tbsp. maple syrup
- 1 large egg
- 2 cups all-purpose flour
- 1/2 tsp. baking soda
- 1/4 tsp. table salt
  Maple-Praline Frosting
- 48 pecan halves, lightly toasted

1. Beat butter and shortening at medium speed with an electric mixer until creamy; gradually add sugar, beating until light and fluffy. Add maple syrup and egg, beating until blended.
2. Stir together flour, baking soda, and salt; gradually add to butter mixture, beating until blended. Cover and chill dough 1 hour.
3. Preheat oven to 350°. Drop dough by rounded tablespoonfuls onto ungreased baking sheets.
4. Bake at 350° for 9 to 10 minutes or until edges are lightly browned. Cool on baking sheets 1 minute. Transfer to wire racks, and cool completely (about 10 minutes).
5. Spread Maple-Praline Frosting over cookies. Top each cookie with 1 pecan half.

Maple-Praline Frosting

Makes: 1 cup
Hands-On Time: 12 min. Total Time: 12 min.

- 1 cup firmly packed light brown sugar
- 1/3 cup whipping cream
- 2 Tbsp. maple syrup
- 1 cup powdered sugar

Combine brown sugar and whipping cream in a 2-qt. saucepan. Cook over medium heat, stirring constantly, until mixture comes to a boil; boil 4 minutes (do not stir). Remove from heat; stir in maple syrup. Gradually stir in powdered sugar until smooth. Use immediately. If frosting hardens, stir in additional whipping cream, 1/2 tsp. at a time, as needed.

Almond Poinsettia Cookies

(pictured on page 147)

Makes: about 2 1/2 dozen
Hands-On Time: 1 hour Total Time: 4 hours, 25 min.

This recipe bakes up into beautiful flower shapes that are ready for decorating. Shop online for a poinsettia cookie cutter.

- 2 cups all-purpose flour
- 1/2 cup almond flour
- 1/4 tsp. table salt
- 3/4 cup butter, softened
- 2 oz. cream cheese, softened
- 2 oz. almond paste
- 1 cup granulated sugar
- 1 large egg yolk
- 1 tsp. almond extract
  Royal Red Icing
- 1/4 cup yellow candy sprinkles
- 1/4 cup fine red sanding sugar

1. Combine first 3 ingredients in a small bowl. Beat butter and cream cheese at medium speed with an electric mixer until creamy. Add almond paste and granulated sugar, beating until light and fluffy. Add egg yolk and almond extract, beating just until blended. Gradually add flour mixture to cream cheese mixture, beating just until blended after each addition.
2. Divide dough into 2 equal portions; flatten each into a disk. Cover and chill 2 hours.
3. Preheat oven to 350°. Place 1 portion of dough on a lightly floured surface, and roll to a 1/4-inch thickness. Cut with a 3 1/2- to 4-inch poinsettia cookie cutter. Place cookies 1 inch apart on ungreased baking sheets. Repeat procedure with remaining dough disk.
4. Bake at 350° for 13 to 15 minutes or until edges are golden brown. Cool on baking sheets 2 minutes. Transfer to wire racks, and cool completely (about 30 minutes).
5. Spoon Royal Red Icing into a small zip-top plastic freezer bag. Snip 1 corner of bag to make a small hole. Working with 1 cookie at a time, pipe icing to outline cookie. Use icing to fill in cookie. Lightly sprinkle yellow candies in center. Sprinkle petals with red sugar.

Royal Red Icing

Makes: about 3 cups
Hands-On Time: 10 min. Total Time: 10 min.

- 1 (16-oz.) package powdered sugar
- 3 Tbsp. meringue powder
- 3/4 tsp. red paste food color
- 4 to 6 Tbsp. warm water

Beat first 3 ingredients and 4 Tbsp. water at low speed with an electric mixer until blended. Add up to 2 Tbsp. additional water, 1 tsp. at a time, until desired consistency is reached.

NOTE: Royal Icing dries rapidly. Work quickly, keeping extra icing tightly covered at all times. Place a damp paper towel directly on surface of icing (to prevent a crust from forming) while icing cookies.

White Chocolate-Peppermint Cookies

Makes: 2 dozen
Hands-On Time: 25 min. Total Time: 45 min.

1/2	cup sugar
6	Tbsp. butter, softened
1	large egg
1/2	tsp. peppermint extract
1 1/4	cups all-purpose flour
1/2	tsp. baking powder
1/4	tsp. table salt
23	hard peppermint candies, crushed and divided
	Parchment paper
2	Tbsp. vegetable shortening
2	(4-oz.) bars white chocolate, chopped

1. Beat sugar and butter at medium speed with an electric mixer 2 minutes or until fluffy. Add egg and peppermint extract, beating just until blended.

2. Stir together flour and next 2 ingredients; gradually add to butter mixture, beating just until blended. Stir in 1/3 cup (about 13) finely crushed candies.

3. Shape dough into 2 logs (about 2 inches in diameter); wrap each log in plastic wrap. Freeze 45 minutes or until firm.

4. Preheat oven to 350°. Cut each log into 1/4-inch-thick slices; place on parchment paper-lined baking sheets. Bake at 350° for 10 minutes or until lightly browned. Remove from baking sheets to wire racks, and cool completely (about 20 minutes).

5. Place shortening and chocolate in a medium bowl. Microwave at MEDIUM 1 minute or until chocolate melts and mixture is smooth, stirring every 30 seconds.

6. Spoon chocolate mixture over cookies to coat tops. Place onto parchment-lined baking sheets. Sprinkle with remaining crushed candies. Let stand until chocolate is firm.

Pistachio Meringue Kisses

Makes: 6 dozen
Hands-On Time: 30 min. Total Time: 5 hours, 30 min.
Sweet meringue kisses get a flavor boost from the addition
of chopped pistachios and bittersweet chocolate-dipped
bottoms. These pretty treats will be the star of your holiday
cookie tray.

> 3 **large egg whites**
> ¼ **tsp. cream of tartar**
> ¼ **tsp. vanilla extract**
> ⅛ **tsp. table salt**
> ½ **cup granulated sugar**
> ¾ **cup finely chopped pistachios, divided**
> 1 **Tbsp. powdered sugar**
> **Parchment paper**
> 1 **(6-oz.) bittersweet chocolate baking bar, chopped**

1. Preheat oven to 175°. Beat first 4 ingredients at high speed with
an electric mixer until foamy. Gradually add granulated sugar,
1 Tbsp. at a time, beating until stiff peaks form and sugar dissolves
(about 2 to 4 minutes). Stir together ½ cup pistachios and
powdered sugar; fold into meringue.
2. Insert metal tip #827 (star tip) into a large decorating bag; fill
with meringue. Pipe meringue into 72 (1-inch) mounds onto
2 parchment paper-lined baking sheets. Sprinkle with remaining
¼ cup pistachios.
3. Bake at 175° for 3 hours or until meringues are dry to the touch.
(Meringues are done when surface is dry and meringues can be
removed from paper without sticking to fingers.) Turn oven off;
let meringues stand in closed oven 1 hour. Remove from oven,
and cool completely (about 45 minutes). Remove meringues from
parchment paper; keep parchment paper.
4. Microwave chocolate in microwave-safe bowl at HIGH 1 to
1½ minutes or until melted and smooth, stirring at 30-second
intervals. Dip bottoms of meringues in melted chocolate. Return
to parchment paper; let stand until chocolate is firm.

Ruby Red Grapefruit Bars

Makes: 2 dozen
Hands-On Time: 18 min. Total Time: 2 hours, 28 min.

If you would like your bars pink like a fresh-cut grapefruit,
add a drop or two of red food coloring.

- 1 **cup butter, softened**
- ½ **cup powdered sugar**
- 1½ **cups all-purpose flour**
- ⅛ **tsp. table salt**
- 2 **cups granulated sugar**
- ⅓ **cup all-purpose flour**
- ½ **tsp. baking powder**
- 1 **Tbsp. red grapefruit zest**
- ¾ **cup fresh red grapefruit juice**
- 6 **large eggs**
  Christmas stencils (optional)
  Powdered sugar

1. Preheat oven to 350°. Beat butter at medium speed with an electric mixer until creamy; gradually add ½ cup powdered sugar, beating until blended. Add 1½ cups flour and salt; beat until blended. Press mixture into bottom of an ungreased 13- x 9-inch baking pan. Bake at 350° for 18 minutes or until lightly browned. Let cool 10 minutes.

2. Meanwhile, stir together granulated sugar, ⅓ cup flour, and baking powder in a medium bowl. Whisk together zest, juice, and eggs; add to flour mixture, stirring until well blended. Pour over crust.

3. Bake at 350° for 30 minutes or until set. Remove to wire rack, and cool completely (about 1½ hours). Cut into 24 squares, and, if desired, place Christmas stencils over each square; dust with powdered sugar.

Christmas Tree Shortbread

Makes: about 5 dozen
Hands-On Time: 50 min. Total Time: 6 hours

This simple dough can be made ahead to allow more time for holiday shopping and socializing.

- 1 **cup butter, softened**
- ½ **cup sugar**
- 2 **tsp. vanilla extract**
- 2¼ **cups all-purpose flour**
- ¼ **tsp. table salt**
- 6 **Tbsp. small white nonpareils**
  Wax paper
- 1 **(7-oz.) pouch white decorating cookie icing**
  Large yellow and blue star sprinkles

1. Beat butter at medium speed with an electric mixer until creamy. Gradually add sugar, beating until smooth. Stir in vanilla.
2. Stir together flour and salt. Gradually add flour mixture to butter mixture, beating at low speed until blended. Divide dough in half. Shape each portion into a 7-inch log on a lightly floured surface. Place nonpareils in a shallow dish; roll logs in nonpareils, pressing candies gently into logs. Wrap each log in wax paper, and chill 4 hours.
3. Preheat oven to 375°. Cut logs into ¼-inch-thick slices. Place 1 inch apart on lightly greased baking sheets.
4. Bake at 375° for 9 minutes or until set. Transfer to wire racks, and cool completely (about 15 minutes).
5. Place round tip on cookie icing. Pipe icing to outline tree shape on each cookie. Immediately place 1 star sprinkle at top of each tree.

NOTE: Dough logs may be wrapped and frozen in zip-top plastic freezer bags up to 1 month. If frozen, let logs stand at room temperature 15 minutes before slicing and baking.

Love It? GET IT!

Many items pictured in the book are one-of-a-kind or no longer available—we've listed similar looks when possible. Source information is current at the time of publication. If an item is not listed, its source is unknown.

- pages 10-11—**red checked charger:** At Home with Marieke, www.mimexusa.com; **wooden tags:** Anthropologie, www.anthropologie.com
- page 12—**tray:** At Home with Marieke, www.mimexusa.com
- pages 14-15—**flatware:** Pottery Barn, www.potterybarn.com; **skillets:** Le Creuset, www.lecreuset.com
- page 16—**platter:** Vietri, www.vietri.com
- pages 18-19—**glasses:** Roost, www.roostco.com and Juliska, www.juliska.com; **pinecones:** Pottery Barn, www.potterybarn.com; **flatware:** "Fairfax" by Gorham
- page 20—**glasses:** Roost, www.roostco.com
- pages 28-29—**flatware, plate:** Vietri, www.vietri.com
- pages 32-33—**serving dish:** EigenArts, eigenarts.com; **charger:** Vietri, www.vietri.com
- page 35—**linen:** Pottery Barn, www.potterybarn.com
- page 49—**candlesticks:** Pottery Barn, www.potterybarn.com
- pages 50-51—**red yarn tree:** Target, www.target.com; **buckets:** Park Hill Collection, www.parkhillcollection.com; **mugs:** Vietri, www.vietri.com
- page 60—**wreath:** Ballard Designs, www.ballarddesigns.com
- pages 64-65—**burlap and rope trees:** Ballard Designs, www.ballarddesigns.com; **mirror:** Hobby Lobby, www.hobbylobby.com

- page 73—**plates:** Roost, www.roostco.com; **striped napkin:** Fog Linen Work, www.shop-foglinen.com
- pages 74-75—**glass reindeer:** Roost, www.roostco.com; **birch logs and discs:** Wilson Evergreens, www.wilsonevergreens.com
- page 77—**silver candlesticks, white wooden tray, round silver tray:** Nkuku, www.nkuku.com
- pages 78-79—**terrarium:** Hobby Lobby, www.hobbylobby.com
- pages 84-85—**collapsible tree:** West Elm, www.westelm.com
- page 88—**gold plate:** Anthropologie, www.anthropologie.com
- page 101—**cutting board:** J.K. Adams, www.jkadams.com
- page 129—**stars & tray:** Pottery Barn, www.potterybarn.com
- page 135—**pie plate:** Williams Sonoma, www.williams-sonoma.com
- page 141—**napkin:** Pehr Designs, www.pehrdesigns.com
- pages 146-147—**tray:** Mud, Australia, www.mudaustralia.com
- page 150—**measuring spoons:** West Elm, www.westelm.com
- page 154—**dish:** Mud, Australia, www.mudaustralia.com
- page 158—**papers:** Martha Stewart Crafts for Michaels, www.michaels.com
- pages 168-169—**Santa plate:** Vietri, www.vietri.com; **mug:** Anthropologie, www.anthropologie.com

Thanks to these CONTRIBUTORS

Thanks to the following businesses

A'Mano	Davis Wholesale Florist, Inc.	Smith's Variety
Anthropologie	Harmony Landing	Table Matters
At Home	Lamb's Ears, Ltd.	Tricia's Treasures
Bellewether	Leaf & Petal	West Elm
Bromberg's	Oak Street Garden Shop	Williams-Sonoma
Collier's Nursery	Pottery Barn	

Thanks to the following homeowners

Geoff & Tricia Goldens

Harry & Kari Kampakis

Lynn & Duane Randleman

Cotton & Melinda Shallcross

General Index

Metric Equivalents

The recipes that appear in this cookbook use the standard United States method for measuring liquid and dry or solid ingredients (teaspoons, tablespoons, and cups). The information in the following charts is provided to help cooks outside the U.S. successfully use these recipes. All equivalents are approximate.

Metric Equivalents for Different Types of Ingredients

A standard cup measure of a dry or solid ingredient will vary in weight depending on the type of ingredient. A standard cup of liquid is the same volume for any type of liquid. Use the following chart when converting standard cup measures to grams (weight) or milliliters (volume).

Standard Cup	Fine Powder (ex. flour)	Grain (ex. rice)	Granular (ex. sugar)	Liquid Solids (ex. butter)	Liquid (ex. milk)
1	140 g	150 g	190 g	200 g	240 ml
¾	105 g	113 g	143 g	150 g	180 ml
⅔	93 g	100 g	125 g	133 g	160 ml
½	70 g	75 g	95 g	100 g	120 ml
⅓	47 g	50 g	63 g	67 g	80 ml
¼	35 g	38 g	48 g	50 g	60 ml
⅛	18 g	19 g	24 g	25 g	30 ml

Useful Equivalents for Dry Ingredients by Weight
(To convert ounces to grams, multiply the number of ounces by 30.)

1 oz	=	1/16 lb	=	30 g
4 oz	=	¼ lb	=	120 g
8 oz	=	½ lb	=	240 g
12 oz	=	¾ lb	=	360 g
16 oz	=	1 lb	=	480 g

Useful Equivalents for Length
(To convert inches to centimeters, multiply the number of inches by 2.5.)

1 in				=	2.5 cm		
6 in	=	½ ft		=	15 cm		
12 in	=	1 ft		=	30 cm		
36 in	=	3 ft	=	1 yd	=	90 cm	
40 in				=	100 cm	=	1 m

Useful Equivalents for Liquid Ingredients by Volume

¼ tsp					=	1 ml	
½ tsp					=	2 ml	
1 tsp					=	5 ml	
3 tsp	=	1 Tbsp		= ½ fl oz	=	15 ml	
		2 Tbsp	= ⅛ cup	= 1 fl oz	=	30 ml	
		4 Tbsp	= ¼ cup	= 2 fl oz	=	60 ml	
		5⅓ Tbsp	= ⅓ cup	= 3 fl oz	=	80 ml	
		8 Tbsp	= ½ cup	= 4 fl oz	=	120 ml	
		10⅔ Tbsp	= ⅔ cup	= 5 fl oz	=	160 ml	
		12 Tbsp	= ¾ cup	= 6 fl oz	=	180 ml	
		16 Tbsp	= 1 cup	= 8 fl oz	=	240 ml	
	1 pt =	2 cups		= 16 fl oz	=	480 ml	
	1 qt =	4 cups		= 32 fl oz	=	960 ml	
				33 fl oz	=	1000 ml	= 1 l

Useful Equivalents for Cooking/Oven Temperatures

	Fahrenheit	Celsius	Gas Mark
Freeze water	32° F	0° C	
Room temperature	68° F	20° C	
Boil water	212° F	100° C	
Bake	325° F	160° C	3
	350° F	180° C	4
	375° F	190° C	5
	400° F	200° C	6
	425° F	220° C	7
	450° F	230° C	8
Broil			Grill

Recipe Index

©2013 by Time Home Entertainment Inc.
135 West 50th Street, New York, NY 10020

ISBN-13: 978-0-8487-3966-9
ISBN-10: 0-8487-3966-3
ISSN: 0747-7791
Printed in the United States of America
First Printing 2013

Oxmoor House
Editorial Director: Leah McLaughlin
Creative Director: Felicity Keane
Senior Brand Manager: Daniel Fagan
Senior Editor: Rebecca Brennan
Managing Editor: Rebecca Benton

Christmas with Southern Living 2013
Editor: Ashley Strickland Freeman
Assistant Editor: Allison E. Cox
Art Director: Claire Cormany
Project Editor: Megan McSwain Yeatts
Director, Test Kitchen: Elizabeth Tyler Austin
Assistant Directors, Test Kitchen: Julie Christopher, Julie Gunter
Recipe Developers and Testers: Wendy Ball, R.D.; Victoria E. Cox; Tamara
    Goldis; Stefanie Maloney; Callie Nash; Karen Rankin; Leah Van Deren
Recipe Editor: Alyson Moreland Haynes
Food Stylists: Margaret Monroe Dickey, Catherine Crowell Steele
Photography Director: Jim Bathie
Senior Photographer: Helene Dujardin
Senior Photo Stylist: Kay E. Clarke
Photo Stylist: Mindi Shapiro Levine
Assistant Photo Stylist: Mary Louise Menendez
Senior Production Managers: Greg A. Amason, Susan Chodakiewicz

Contributors
Editor: Katherine Cobbs
Designers: Carol Damsky, Nancy Johnson
Recipe Developers and Testers: Erica Hopper, Tonya Johnson,
    Kyra Moncrief, Kathleen Royal Phillips
Copy Editors: Donna Baldone, Stephanie Gibson
Proofreaders: Donna Baldone, Polly Linthicum
Indexer: Mary Ann Laurens
Interns: Megan Branagh, Frances Gunnells, Susan Kemp,
    Staley McIlwain, Jeffrey Preis, Maria Sanders, Julia Sayers
Photographers: Iain Bagwell, Beau Gustafson, Becky Luigart-Stayner,
    Daniel Taylor
Prop Stylists: Ginny Branch, Missie Neville Crawford
Food Stylist: William Smith
Recipe Developer and Tester: Kathleen Royal Phillips
Creative Projects Coordinator: Sara Lyon

Southern Living®
Editor: M. Lindsay Bierman
Creative Director: Robert Perino
Managing Editor: Candace Higginbotham
Art Director: Chris Hoke
Executive Editors: Rachel Hardage Barrett, Hunter Lewis,
    Jessica S. Thuston
Food Director: Shannon Sliter Satterwhite
Test Kitchen Director: Robby Melvin
Senior Food Editor: Mary Allen Perry
Recipe Editor: JoAnn Weatherly
Test Kitchen Specialist/Food Styling: Vanessa McNeil Rocchio
Test Kitchen Professionals: Norman King, Pam Lolley,
    Angela Sellers
Homes Editor: Jennifer Kopf
Decorating Editor: Lindsey Ellis Beatty
Director, Editorial Licensing: Katie Terrell Morrow
Assistant Homes Editor: Zoë Gowen
Photographers: Robbie Caponetto, Laurey W. Glenn, Hector Sanchez
Style Director: Heather Chadduck Hillegas
Senior Photo Stylist: Buffy Hargett
Studio Assistant: Caroline Murphy Cunningham
Editorial Assistants: Marian Cooper, Stephanie Granada, Pat York

Time Home Entertainment Inc.
Publisher: Jim Childs
VP, Brand and Digital Strategy: Steven Sandonato
Executive Director, Marketing Services: Carol Pittard
Executive Director, Retail & Special Sales: Tom Mifsud
Director, Bookazine Development & Marketing: Laura Adam
Executive Publishing Director: Joy Butts
Associate Publishing Director: Megan Pearlman
Finance Director: Glenn Buonocore
Associate General Counsel: Helen Wan

To order additional publications, call 1-800-765-6400 or
    1-800-491-0551.

For more books to enrich your life, visit **oxmoorhouse.com**

To search, savor, and share thousands of recipes, visit **myrecipes.com**

Cover: Mini Red Velvet Cakes with Mascarpone Frosting, page 132

Back Cover: Pretzel-Toffee-Chocolate Chunk Cookies, page 149;
    Favorite Things, page 44; Roast Turkey and Brown Gravy, page 97

Holiday PLANNER

From decorating your house to cooking a holiday feast, this holiday planner helps you get organized and ready for each day leading up to the New Year. Refer to it next year when Christmas time rolls around again!

November 2013

Sunday	Monday	Tuesday	Wednesday
3	4	5	6
10	11	12	13
17	18	19	20
24	25	26	27

Thursday	Friday	Saturday
	1	2
7	8	9
14	15	16
21	22	23
Thanksgiving 28	29	30

Keeping Christmas Fresh

A Healthy and Fresh Christmas Tree

☐ The best way to achieve this is to cut your own tree.

☐ If you can't cut your own tree, carefully examine the tree before purchasing. The needles should be soft and supple with a rich, vibrant color and no hint of yellow.

☐ When you're back home, cut an inch off the bottom of the trunk and immediately plunge it into a bucket of water.

☐ Fir trees last the longest.

Keeping Greenery Fresh

☐ Before buying from the florist or tree lot, check your yard to see if you have any greenery.

☐ Soak the greenery in water overnight before using it.

☐ Once it's dry, spray it with an antidessicant like Wilt-Pruf to lock in the moisture.

☐ Wilt-Pruf is organic, nontoxic, and dries clear. You can find it at most garden centers.

Add Color to Your Greenery

☐ Firm berries last much longer than soft, juicy ones. Nandina lasts forever and the bright-red color really pops.

☐ Deciduous hollies, like winterberry and possumhaw, work great too.

☐ Avoid yaupon and pyracantha berries; they drop quickly indoors.

Doubling the Life of Paperwhites

☐ Give them bright, indirect light and keep them as cool as possible.

☐ Place them outside at night when the temperature won't drop below 35 degrees; they'll stay shorter and last twice as long.

December 2013

Sunday	Monday	Tuesday	Wednesday
1	2	3	4
8	9	10	11
15	16	17	18
22	23	Christmas Eve 24	Christmas 25
29	30	New Year's Eve 31	

	Thursday	Friday	Saturday
	5	6	7
	12	13	14
	19	20	21
	26	27	28

Creating Your Holiday Look

☐ Group similar items and collections for greater impact and less clutter. For example, a cluster of white stoneware pitchers filled with branches of berries makes more of a statement than the same arrangements scattered around the house.

☐ Make it personal. Always use some of your heirloom ornaments, photographs, or collectibles from the past.

☐ Add one new festive element each year to keep your look fresh and updated.

☐ Always use fresh greenery, berries, and fruit for the most beautiful and fragrant holiday embellishments.

☐ A roll of ribbon goes a long way for holiday decorating. You can find ribbons in an array of colors to suit your holiday decor.

☐ Coordinate your wrapping with your tree. Using the same ribbon on your gifts and winding it through the branches of the tree gives a polished look.

Decorating PLANNER

Here's a list of details and finishing touches you can use to tailor a picture-perfect house this holiday season.

Decorative materials needed

from the yard

from around the house

from the store

other

Holiday decorations

for the table

for the door

for the mantel

for the staircase

other

Deck the Hall with Natural Style

Rosemary

Fill your home with the woodsy beauty and distinct fragrance of this fresh herb.
• Trim a tabletop tree. A topiary is a great present that lasts all year, offering tender shoots of herbs that you can add to your favorite recipes.
• Gather an evergreen bouquet. A festive swag on the front door sends a gardener's greeting of Christmas cheer.
• Adorn your gifts with sprigs of fresh rosemary by entwining a fragrant sprig within the ribbon.

Citrus

Add some sunshine to your holiday decor with fruit.
• Trim a fruit tree and make it the focal point on your table display. Tie satin bows around its trunk and surround it with other types of citrus for a fresh, abundant display.
• Dress a window with citrus such as lemons. They are just the right size and weight to adorn an arrangement of boxwood branches and eucalyptus.

• Substitute an arrangement of citrus for flowers for an easy, long-lasting centerpiece. Use extra leaves to fill in gaps, and add a lime or two to amplify the green effect.

Cranberries

Very merry berries add a splash of color all through the house.
• Highlight a tabletop collection of festive glass jugs with colorful garlands of fresh cranberries.
• Thread a large needle with clear fishing line, and string fresh cranberries. Drape the finished product like a necklace over a bust.
• Spruce up an evergreen wreath by wrapping white ribbon and strung cranberries around the wreath twice, layering over the ribbon.
• Plant an amaryllis bulb in a narrow glass vase. Carefully place the narrow vase inside a large one, filling the empty space between with cranberries.

INSTANT WAYS TO Trim Your Tree

This Christmas create elegant additions around your house that are tailored to add some holiday flair. Here are some tips and hints on how to give your tree a fresh, new look and maintain the spirit of Christmas.

• ***Go vintage*** with a mix of retro-chic glass ornaments in bright colors and stripes.

• ***Bunch several ornaments together*** and top with a wide satin ribbon. For an extra pop of color, string fresh cranberries as garland.

• ***Highlight your tree's graceful form*** by draping its branches with colorful ribbon.

• ***Mix favorite family collectibles*** with festive glass spheres. Fun souvenirs from a few memorable vacations or even your home turf take on a classic look when paired with modern trimmings.

• ***Adorn your tree with natural elements*** such as birch disks and dried flowers.

• ***Add a live element*** by placing sprigs of fresh flowers in hanging vases.

• ***Pair fresh pink bougainvillea*** with silvery sage and dusty miller to make beautiful, rosy bouquets. Small shiny orbs attached with florist wire reflect the tree lights for some extra sparkle.

MAKE A Mistletoe Kissing Ball

So much better than holding a spindly twig over someone's head, this creation is a beautiful holiday decoration. Make extras to give to special friends.

Supplies you'll need:

4½-inch florist foam ball
24-gauge wire
garden shears
sheet moss
20 to 30 branches of mistletoe
3½-inch pearl florist pins
38-inch-long ribbon

1. Soak the florist foam ball in water. Submerge it for 15 minutes until it's saturated.

2. Cut the floral wire into 1½-inch strips. Bend the pieces into a U-shape.

3. Cover the moistened ball with sheet moss. Secure the moss with the floral wire.

4. Cut mistletoe into 2- to 3-inch pieces. Adhere by pushing the mistletoe stems through the sheet moss and directly into the foam ball. (For less sturdy stems, create small holes with an ice pick before inserting the stems into the ball.) Heads up: You may need up to 150 small pieces to fully cover the florist foam ball.

5. Push florist pins into the foam ball to create a pearly decoration. Place as desired for additional decoration.

6. Add a bow. Starting at one end of the ribbon, fold a 10-inch loop (this will be what you use to hang the ball), and then fold two 8-inch loops. This will leave you with a 12-inch tail of ribbon. Cut 6 inches off the tail and lay it on the opposite side of the loops. Pinch the loops and tail together at the center, and secure with a 16-inch piece of wire bent in half. Firmly twist the wire until you create a stem sturdy enough to insert in the mistletoe ball.

Party PLANNER

Keep track of your holiday menu with this time-saving chart.

GUESTS	WHAT THEY'RE BRINGING	SERVING PIECES NEEDED
....	☐ appetizer ☐ beverage ☐ bread ☐ main dish ☐ side dish ☐ dessert	....
....	☐ appetizer ☐ beverage ☐ bread ☐ main dish ☐ side dish ☐ dessert	....
....	☐ appetizer ☐ beverage ☐ bread ☐ main dish ☐ side dish ☐ dessert	....
....	☐ appetizer ☐ beverage ☐ bread ☐ main dish ☐ side dish ☐ dessert	....
....	☐ appetizer ☐ beverage ☐ bread ☐ main dish ☐ side dish ☐ dessert	....
....	☐ appetizer ☐ beverage ☐ bread ☐ main dish ☐ side dish ☐ dessert	
....	☐ appetizer ☐ beverage ☐ bread ☐ main dish ☐ side dish ☐ dessert	....
....	☐ appetizer ☐ beverage ☐ bread ☐ main dish ☐ side dish ☐ dessert	....
....	☐ appetizer ☐ beverage ☐ bread ☐ main dish ☐ side dish ☐ dessert	....
....	☐ appetizer ☐ beverage ☐ bread ☐ main dish ☐ side dish ☐ dessert	....
....	☐ appetizer ☐ beverage ☐ bread ☐ main dish ☐ side dish ☐ dessert	....
....	☐ appetizer ☐ beverage ☐ bread ☐ main dish ☐ side dish ☐ dessert	....
....	☐ appetizer ☐ beverage ☐ bread ☐ main dish ☐ side dish ☐ dessert	....
....	☐ appetizer ☐ beverage ☐ bread ☐ main dish ☐ side dish ☐ dessert	....
....	☐ appetizer ☐ beverage ☐ bread ☐ main dish ☐ side dish ☐ dessert	....

Party Guest List

Pantry List

Party To-Do List

Christmas Dinner PLANNER

Gather your thoughts and ideas for menu ideas, dinner to-do lists,
and guest lists on this holiday meal planner.

Menu Ideas

Dinner To-Do List

Christmas Dinner Guest List

Mix-and-Match MENUS

Menus below are based on recipes in the book.

Traditional Christmas Dinner

Southern Green Beans (page 23)

Roast Turkey and Brown Gravy (page 97)

Winter Citrus-Avocado Salad (page 115)

Mocha-Hazelnut Dacquoise (page 136)

Serves 8 to 10

Winter Repast

Oyster-and-Wild Rice Bisque (page 95)

Pumpkin Soup with Red Pepper Relish (page 93)

Pomegranate Roasted Duck Breast (page 107)

Simple Herbed Gravy with Egg (page 101)

Gingered Bread Pudding with Limoncello Cream Sauce (page 35)

Serves 8

Meat-and-Potatoes Supper

Tuscan Beef Tenderloin (page 105)

Sweet Potato Cloverleaf Rolls (page 24)

Bacon-Apple Gravy (page 101)

Potato Gratin with Bacon and Comté (page 113)

Salted Caramel Black Bottom Cheesecake (page 131)

Serves 8 to 10

Fit for a King

Crown Pork Roast with Fig-Fennel Stuffing (page 103)

Pear-and-Blue Cheese Salad (x2) (page 113)

Crab Arancini (page 34)

Savory Pancetta-Gruyère Rolls (page 127)

Mini Brie en Croûte (page 21)

Stacked Apples (page 26)

Champagne

Serves 12

Party Time

Champagne Cocktail (page 21)

Winter Sangria (page 89)

Ruby Red Negroni (x2) (page 89)

Cranberry-Chutney Cheese Ball (page 90)

White German Chocolate Cake (page 138)

Cream Liqueur-Spiked Coffee (x2) (page 13)

Serves 8 to 10

Food for Comfort

Cane Syrup-and-Black Pepper Bacon (page 13)

Sage Biscuits and Sausage Gravy (page 17)

Pork Chops with Bourbon-Rosemary-Mustard Sauce (page 39)

Pecan Cornbread (page 40)

Cranberry Congealed Salad (page 25)

Southern Anadama Bread (page 129)

Serves 6 to 8

Gifts AND Greetings

Keep up with family & friends' sizes, jot down gift ideas, and record purchases in this convenient chart. Also use it to keep track of addresses for your Christmas card list.

Gift List and Size Charts

NAME/SIZES	GIFT PURCHASED/MADE	SENT/DELIVERED

name..

jeans_____ shirt_____ sweater_____ jacket_____ shoes_____ belt_____

blouse_____ skirt_____ slacks_____ dress_____ suit_____ coat_____

pajamas_____ robe_____ hat_____ gloves_____ ring_____

name..

jeans_____ shirt_____ sweater_____ jacket_____ shoes_____ belt_____

blouse_____ skirt_____ slacks_____ dress_____ suit_____ coat_____

pajamas_____ robe_____ hat_____ gloves_____ ring_____

name..

jeans_____ shirt_____ sweater_____ jacket_____ shoes_____ belt_____

blouse_____ skirt_____ slacks_____ dress_____ suit_____ coat_____

pajamas_____ robe_____ hat_____ gloves_____ ring_____

name..

jeans_____ shirt_____ sweater_____ jacket_____ shoes_____ belt_____

blouse_____ skirt_____ slacks_____ dress_____ suit_____ coat_____

pajamas_____ robe_____ hat_____ gloves_____ ring_____

name..

jeans_____ shirt_____ sweater_____ jacket_____ shoes_____ belt_____

blouse_____ skirt_____ slacks_____ dress_____ suit_____ coat_____

pajamas_____ robe_____ hat_____ gloves_____ ring_____

name..

jeans_____ shirt_____ sweater_____ jacket_____ shoes_____ belt_____

blouse_____ skirt_____ slacks_____ dress_____ suit_____ coat_____

pajamas_____ robe_____ hat_____ gloves_____ ring_____

name..

jeans_____ shirt_____ sweater_____ jacket_____ shoes_____ belt_____

blouse_____ skirt_____ slacks_____ dress_____ suit_____ coat_____

pajamas_____ robe_____ hat_____ gloves_____ ring_____

Christmas Card List

NAME	ADDRESS	SENT/DELIVERED

HOLIDAY Memories

Hold on to priceless Christmas memories forever with
handwritten recollections of this season's magical moments.

Treasured Traditions

Keep track of your family's favorite holiday customs and pastimes on these lines.

....

....

....

....

....

....

....

....

....

....

....

....

Special Holiday Activities

What holiday events do you look forward to year after year? Write them down here.

....

....

....

....

....

....

....

....

Holiday Visits and Visitors

Keep a list of this year's holiday visitors. Jot down friend and family news as well.

....
....
....
....
....
....
....
....
....
....
....
....
....
....
....
....
....
....
....
....
....
....
....
....
....

This Year's Favorite Recipes

Appetizers and Beverages ....
....
....
....
....

Entrées ....
....
....
....

Sides and Salads ....
....
....
....

Cookies and Candies ....
....
....

Desserts ....
....
....

Looking AHEAD

Holiday Wrap-up

Use this checklist to record thank-you notes sent for holiday gifts and hospitality.

NAME	GIFT AND/OR EVENT	NOTE SENT
		☐
		☐
		☐
		☐
		☐
		☐
		☐
		☐
		☐
		☐
		☐
		☐
		☐

Notes for Next Year

Write down your ideas for Christmas 2014 on the lines below.